Presenting Java

John December

201 West 103rd Street
Indianapolis, IN 46290

D1417585

For Lorrie LeJeune

Copyright © 1995 by Sams.net Publishing

FIRST EDITION

International Standard Book Number: 1-57521-039-8

Library of Congress Catalog Card Number: 95-74791

98 97 96 95   4 3 2

Interpretation of the printing code: the rightmost double-digit number is the year of the book's printing; the rightmost single-digit, the number of the book's printing. For example, a printing code of 95-1 shows that the first printing of the book occurred in 1995.

Composed in AGaramond and MCPdigital by Macmillan Computer Publishing

Printed in the United States of America

Trademarks

Publisher	*Richard K. Swadley*
Publisher, Sams.net Publishing	*George Bond*
Managing Editor	*Cindy Morrow*
Marketing Manager	*John Pierce*

Acquisitions Editor
Mark Taber

Development and Technical Editor
Lisa Friendly

Copy Editor
Mitzi Foster Gianakos

Editorial Coordinator
Bill Whitmer

Formatter
Frank Sinclair

Editorial Assistant
Carol Ackerman

Cover Designer
Tim Amrhein

Book Designer
Alyssa Yesh

Production Team Supervisor
Brad Chinn

Production
Angela D. Bannan, Mona Brown, Greg Eldred, Paula Lowell, Kevin Laseau, Casey Price, Nancy Price, Bobbi Satterfield, Tina Trettin

Indexer
Jeanne Clark

Overview

Contents

Acknowledgments

Thanks to everyone at Sams.Net who worked so hard to make this book a reality. Thanks to Mark Taber and George Bond for giving me the opportunity to write this book.

I'd like to thank all the people whose applications I've examined or mentioned. They took the time to answer my questions and continue to create innovative and valuable resources for the Web community as a whole. Thanks to the Java team at Sun Microsystems for creating this new dimension in Web communications.

My colleagues and friends at the Department of Language, Literature, and Communication at Rensselaer Polytechnic Institute have been helpful and supportive. Thanks to my dissertation advisor, Robert Krull, and all the faculty and students in the department for their kind encouragement, patience, and support.

Special thanks also to Dave Hollinger at Rensselaer's Department of Computer Science, the people at Rensselaer's Information Technology Services, and the RPInfo team.

About the Author

John December is a candidate in the Ph.D. program in Communication and Rhetoric at Rensselaer Polytechnic Institute in Troy, New York. Coauthor of *The World Wide Web Unleashed* and *HTML and CGI Unleashed* (both available from Sams.net), he has also written for magazines and journals about the World Wide Web, Internet, and computer-mediated communication. He's widely known on the Net for his Web-based resource lists about the Internet and as publisher of *Computer-Mediated Communication* magazine. He can be reached via the Internet (john@december.com) or web (http://www.december.com/).

Introduction

What do the Rolling Stones and Sun Microsystems have in common? First, both organizations have sites on the World Wide Web to promote their work. Second, each has chosen Java as a new way to enliven their World Wide Web pages.

What is Java?

Java is a programming language developed by Sun Microsystems that brings animation and interaction to the World Wide Web. HotJava is the name of the software developed by Sun that you can use to observe and interact with Java programs. Java unleashes a level of interactivity that has never been possible on the Web. This book explores and introduces you to Java's potential for distributing interactive, executable content.

People and organizations use the World Wide Web to communicate globally and instantly. Using the Internet as a network for data transfer, the Web employs a form of expression called hypertext that connects related information in web-like structures. Combined with multimedia, the resulting webs of hypermedia have opened new possibilities for expression and communication.

But something has been missing from the Web since its introduction to the world in the early 1990s. Although the amount of Web data traffic and the number of computers offering information on the Web has risen dramatically, the *content* of the pages has lacked important expressive and interactive qualities. While often intriguing, informative, and useful, Web content has been devoid of the degree of interactivity offered by many multimedia and hypermedia systems that run on non-networked computers. So although the Web fostered world-wide interconnections among people and information, it has only enabled people to observe: read text, watch videos, listen to music, and explore information.

The unbounded universe of possibilities on the Web may lead some users to feel that the hyperlinks just keep leading them on, until ultimately, the Web seems just a road to nowhere: with no *there* there. Java changes all this. Java makes *destinations* possible for Web users.

Java enables developers to create content that can be delivered to and run by users on their computers. This software can support anything that programmers can dream up: spreadsheets, tutorials, animations, and interactive games. With the Web page as the delivery platform, this software can support a variety of information tasks with true interactivity; users can get continuous, instantaneous feedback for applications in visualization, animation and computation.

Users of the Web in the dawning Java age may indeed find a *there* on the Web: a place to play, work, or learn.

Why Java?

Java is just one part of the integrated set of systems that support World Wide Web communication. Java is an entirely separate programming language from the markup scheme for defining hypertext, the Hypertext Markup Language (HTML). Java doesn't replace HTML, nor does it negate all current work that has been developed or deployed on the Web.

Java connects with HTML and the Web through a special HTML tag called APP, which allows developers to include special Java programs called *applets* on Web pages. These applets are essentially software programs that the user's browser downloads (automatically, as part of Web page observation) and executes. With graphical input and output possible through the applet on the page, Java thus opens windows into richer levels of interactivity on the Web.

Why This Book?

The purpose of this book is to give you an understanding of what Java is, how it transforms Web communication, and Java's principle technical features.

This book delves into the possibilities Java offers in animation, interaction, and distributed network communication. This book aims to help you:

- Appreciate the profound way Java transforms the World Wide Web
- Grasp conceptually what is involved with using Java, including the HTML-to-Java connection and the roles of the HotJava browser and the Java language
- Learn about the HotJava browser and how to download and use it
- Understand how the Java language works, including the basics of data definition and program control
- Gain insight into how Java follows an object-oriented paradigm that encourages software reusability
- See some example Java applets that support animations, interactivity, and network applications

How to Use This Book

This book is an introduction to Java's essentials: how Java connects with the Web, how to view Java programs, and the basics of constructing Java programs. This book is organized so that users at all levels can traverse it in a variety of paths.

The Scope of This Book

This book discusses the significance of Java and showcases the kinds of applications it makes possible. This book provides a quick overview of the HotJava browser, how to obtain it, and how it can be used to navigate the Web. The book then surveys the main features of the Java language, describing the basics of its procedural programming features and how it supports the object-oriented paradigm. This language description includes many examples—showing the very basics for applets and applications. Finally, the book surveys many existing Java programs and examines what kind of communication they make possible and the basics of how they work.

This book cannot possibly do justice to the rich and very rapid ways that Java is developing technically and expressively. As such, this book is limited in two ways:

1. It covers the alpha release of Java/HotJava that was available in the summer of 1995. A beta release of Java/HotJava is expected for later in 1995. The support web for this book (`http://www.rpi.edu/~decemj/works/java.html`) contains a summary of changes relevant to this book after the beta release is available.

2. This book is not meant to be a comprehensive reference or advanced programming guide for Java. It instead provides a quick start for new users, project planners, and developers, with coverage of introductory conceptual and beginning technical information about Java, with pointers to online locations of full and current reference information.

Organization of This Book

This book is organized into parts, each of which contains three chapters. Each part introduces the essentials of Java from a different perspective, and each chapter in the parts addresses a central main point stated in a declarative sentence as the chapter title. Here is a summary of the contents in these parts:

Part I, "Understanding the Potential of Java and the Web," is an overview of the potential of the Web and Java. These chapters explore Java's capability to deliver distributed, executable content, Java's technical design for flexibility and extensibility, and Java's relationship with the Web as a system of communication for distributing networked hypermedia.

Part II, "Exploring Java's Potential," surveys Java's capabilities for animation, interaction, and information distribution. These chapters discuss many case studies demonstrating Java in action. You can try out some of the examples shown and learn about key code programming techniques of these examples.

Part III, "Using the HotJava Browser," is an overview of the HotJava browser. The first chapter describes how you can download and set up HotJava, Sun Microsystems' demonstration Java-enabled Web browser. The other chapters explore the important difference between HotJava and other Web browsers and how you can use HotJava to navigate the Web.

Part IV introduces the basics of developing Java Programs. These chapters explain Java's procedural features, as well as Java's object-oriented features to support classes. This part concludes with a brief example case study of applet design and implementation.

The appendixes describe sources of further information, a summary of the Java language essentials, as well as other supporting information for Java and Web development. The glossary defines Java- and Web-related terms used throughout this book.

Who Might Use This Book?

- Managers and planners who are interested in seeing what Java technology might do for their organization
- Information developers who want to get an idea of how Java works
- Web developers and programmers who want to see quickly how to expand the level of interactivity of their information with Java
- Students in online communication or hypermedia courses who need to grasp the essentials of Java

How Might You Use This Book?

- If you are a new Internet/Web user: Get an idea of how the Web relates to the Internet and Web with Parts I and II, skipping over the programming features described in Part II. Check out Part III or ask your online service provider or administrator if your computer can support Java-enabled browsers. To start writing Java applets, read Part IV, and then take another look at the applications in Part II.
- If you are a manager/project planner: Chapter 1 summarizes the key concepts of Java's potential for communication. Chapter 2 is a technical summary of Java, and Chapter 3 examines in more detail the relationship of Java to the Web. For planning user access to Java content, you'll need to obtain Java-enabled browsers as described in Part III. For planning or managing programming projects involved with Java, read Parts II and IV.
- If you are a Web developer: Go right to Part II to look at what Java is already making possible on the Web. Find out if your platform supports a Java-enabled browser, and, if possible, get a HotJava browser as described in Part III. Read Part IV for an overview of Java programming. Part I is a summary overview of Java; in particular read Chapter 3's discussion of the relationship of Java to the Web and what new kinds of development Java makes possible.
- If you are an application programmer: Check to see whether your development platform suports HotJava as described in Part III. Chapter 2 and Appendix B are key technical summaries of Java. If your platform supports a Java-enabled browser, try the exercises in Part IV and skim Parts II and I for examples. Use this book's support web to get the latest versions of this source code. Use online information sources listed in Appendix A to get the more detailed information about the Java language specification.

Online Support

Book Support Web

To connect to the latest information about this book's contents, open the URL `http://www.rpi.edu/~decemj/works/java.html`. This support web provides links to online information about the book, code samples, and updates on resources and related information. Check with the errata page of this support web for corrections, and send reports of other errors, questions, or comments to the author at `john@december.com`.

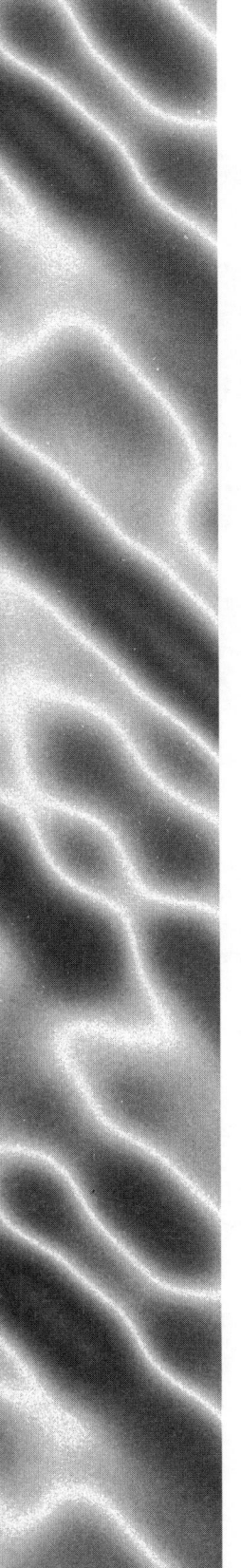

Understanding the Potential of Java and the Web

A great deal of attention was paid to Pizza Hut's October 1994 experiment in product delivery via the Web. Using an interface resembling a fill-in paper form, the Pizza Hut Web site (http://www.pizzahut.com/) could accept orders for pizza. Hungry Web users ordered pizza this way from the small geographical area (Santa Cruz, California) served by the Web and only for a limited time. Yet the ability to send a personal request via a Web page was seen as a major advance, and Pizza Hut's innovative experiment earned the company a great deal of publicity.

Such dreams of ordering pizza marked the state of Web in the pre-Java age. Forms interfaces (for example, shown in Figure P1.1) can accept input from users and then send this information to a Web server program for further processing. This gives the user a way to provide input instead of just selecting and observing information.

But fill-in check boxes and the programming techniques behind processing them have gone only so far toward interactivity. With Forms such as this, the user still receives no real-time response to input. The display of information is also static: because the user must use the mouse to click on something and get a response, the user remains the engine driving the communication; consequently, there are few surprises.

Figure P1.1.
An example of an interactive Form on the Web.

Java changes this static model of Web communication and adds the dimension of interactivity and animation. With the Web's hypertext still serving as a switching mechanism to draw people to a site, Java can give users a way to *do something* at that site: interact with content, be surprised by an animation, or work in a creative way with information. The key to Java's capabilities is *executable content*. The Java language was specifically designed to deliver executable content as well as to be flexible and extensible.

The three chapters in this part explore Java's potential, Java's technical design, and how Java transforms the Web.

These chapters will help give you:

- Knowledge of how Java enriches the Web's interactivity through executable content
- A grasp of how Java technically fits into Web communication and its design as a flexible and dynamic language
- An understanding of how Java transforms the Web's basis as a system for the associative, non-linear organization of information

CHAPTER 1

Java Makes Executable Content Possible

The World Wide Web has transformed the online world. No longer constrained to just text-only information systems, users of the Web have a great deal of choices for selecting and viewing information. The Web's system of hypertext gives users a high degree of selectivity, and hypermedia opens up many options for new kinds of sensory input a user might receive. Using the Web, you can access information, graphics, text, or even videos. However, the Web lacks true interactivity—real-time, dynamic, and visual interaction between the user and application.

Java brings this missing interactivity to the Web. With a Java-enabled Web browser, you can encounter animations and interactive applications. Java programmers can make customized media formats and information protocols that can be displayed in any Java-enabled browser. Java's features enrich the communication, information, and interaction on the Web by enabling users to distribute executable content—rather than just HTML pages and multimedia files—to users. This distribution of executable content is the power of Java.

With origins in Sun Microsystem's work to build a programming language to create software that can run on many different kinds of devices, Java evolved into a language for distributing executable content through the Web. Today, Java brings new interest to Web pages through applications that all can give the user immediate feedback and accept user input continuously through mouse or keyboard entries.

In this chapter, I first present a description and definition of Java and explore what Java brings to Web communication. Then I present a brief "armchair" tour of some examples of what Java can do. If you want to go directly to programming in Java, see Part IV of this book. Otherwise, read this chapter and the next, which survey the potential and the technical side of Java in preparation for the more detailed look at existing Java programs in Part II of this book.

What Can Java Do?

Java animates pages on the Web and makes interactive and specialized applications possible. Figure 1.1 illustrates how the software used with the Web can support a variety of communication. With hypertext, the basis for information organization, you can select what information to view. Programmers can create special kinds of gateway programs that use these files of hypertext on the Web as interfaces. When you use a Web page with such a gateway program associated with it, you can access databases or receive a customized response based on a query. But Java's executable content brings the opportunity for a hypertext page to involve you in continuous, real-time, and complex interaction. This executable content is literally downloaded to your computer so that it can run an animation, perform computation, or guide you through more information at remote network sites.

Figure 1.1.
The Web's software
supports selectivity,
display, computation,
and interactivity.

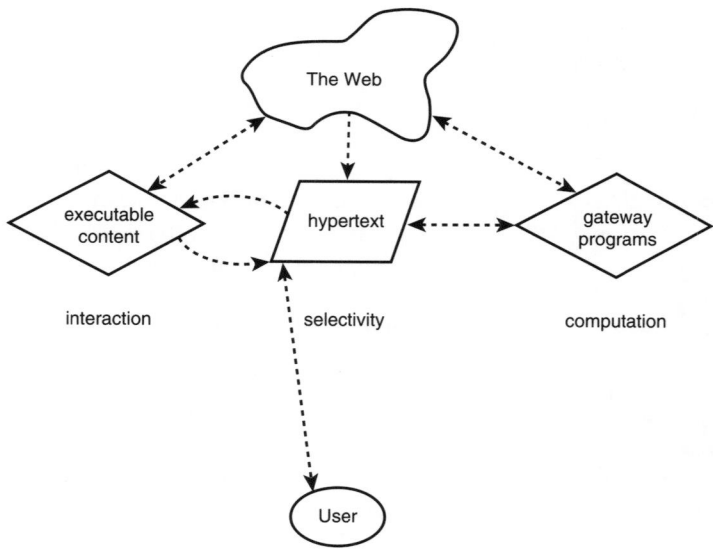

A Metaphor For Java

One metaphor for hypertext is that it offers a visually static page of information (which can include text, graphics, sound, and video). The hypertext page can also have "depth" where it contains hyperlinks connecting to other documents or resources.

Java transforms this static page metaphor into a more dynamic one. The information on a Java page on the Web does not have to be visually static or limited to a pre-defined set of ways to interact with users. Users encountering Java programs can take part in a wider variety of interactive behavior, limited only by the imagination and skill of the Java programmer. Java thus transforms a hypertext page into a stage, complete with the chance for actors and players to appear and things to happen. And, instead of the user being in the audience, you as a user of a Java-enabled Web browser are actively a part of the activity on this stage. With Java, you can take part in changing what transpires and react to it, making you more actively involved in shaping the information content delivered on the Web.

Java thus brings Web pages alive through animation and a higher degree of interaction than what is possible through gateway programming alone.

What Is Java?

The name Java stands for the programming language developed by Sun Microsystems that is used to create executable content that can be distributed through networks. Used generically, the name Java stands for a set of software tools used to create and implement executable content using the Java programming language. One key software tool is the special browser that can interpret Java-generated code. The browser, called HotJava, was developed to showcase the capabilities of the Java programming language.

HotJava has the same capabilities as most Web browsers, but is additionally capable of interpreting and displaying Java's executable content. So while HotJava can display any page on the Web, a Web browser that does not recognize Java can't display the Java executables. Thus, the HotJava browser "sees" the Web plus more—applications written using Java. As described in the following section on Java's origins and future, Java capability is expected to be integrated into future versions of other Web browsers. If you want to obtain and download a HotJava browser now, see Part III of this book.

> ### Java's Home
>
> Sun Microsystems, the developers of Java, provide a one-stop collection of information about Java on the Web at `http://java.sun.com/`. This site includes a full range of the latest information on Java and Java-enabled browsers. Links from this site take you to detailed announcements, release information, documentation, and links to Java demonstrations.

When you download HotJava, the browser, you can also get a set of Java language development tools. Chapter 2 describes this software as well as Java's technical design in more detail.

What Is Executable Content?

Executable content is a general term that identifies the important difference between the content that a Java-enabled Web browser downloads and the content a non-Java-enabled browser can download. Simply put: In a non-Java Web browser, the downloaded content is defined in terms of Multipurpose Internet Mail Extensions (MIME) specifications, which include a variety of multimedia document formats. This specification of content is made so that it can be *displayed* in the browser or in a helper application (to display multimedia such as images, sound, and video). The result is that the user chooses and then observes content.

A Java-enabled browser also downloads content defined by MIME specifications and displays it. However, the key difference is that a Java-enabled browser recognizes a special hypertext item called <CODE>*APP*</CODE>. When downloading a Web page containing APP, the Java-enabled browser knows that a special kind of Java program called an *applet* is associated with that page. The browser then downloads a file of information that describes the execution of that applet. This file of information is written in what are called *bytecodes*. The Java-enabled browser interprets these bytecodes and runs them as an executable program on the user's host. This downloading and execution happens automatically, without requiring the user to request it.

So when surfing the Web with a Java-enabled browser, you might find not only all the hypertext content that the pre-Java age Web offered, but also animated, executable, and distributed content. Moreover, this executable content can include instructions for handling new forms of media as well as information protocols.

How Java Changes the Web

Java profoundly changes the Web because it brings a richness of interactivity and information delivery not possible using previous Web software systems.

Figure 1.2 illustrates the technical difference between Java's interactivity and hypertext selectivity and gateway programming. The figure illustrates how gateway programming allows for computation and response, but not in real time.

Figure 1.2.
Java interactivity is based on executable content downloaded to the user's computer.

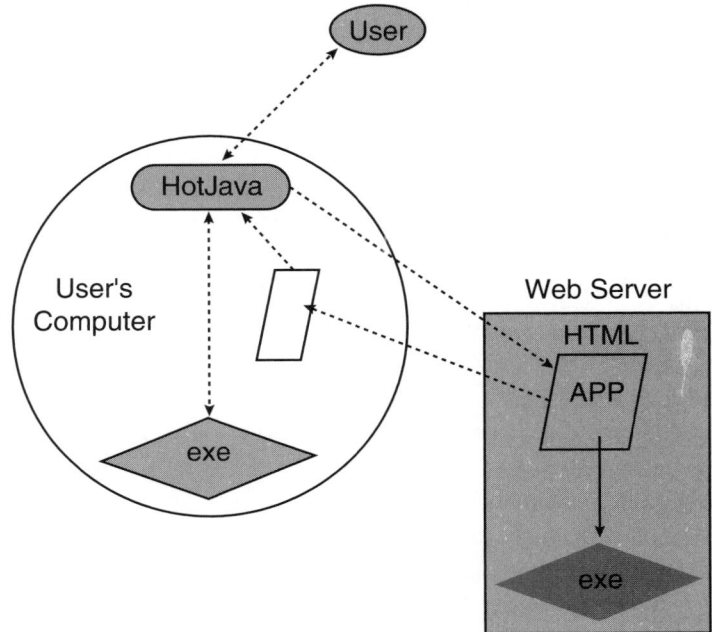

Java Origins and Direction

According to Michael O'Connell's feature article on the origins of Java in the July 7, 1995 issue of *SunWorld Online* (`http://www.sun.com/sunworldonline/swol-07-1995/swol-07-java.html`), the development of Java began at Sun Microsystems in California just as the World Wide Web was being developed in Switzerland in 1991. The goal of this early development team, including Java creator James Gosling, was to develop consumer electronic products that could be simple and bug-free. What was needed was a way to create platform-independent code and thus allow the software to run on any Central Processing Unit (CPU).

As a starting point for a computer language to implement this platform independence, the development team focused first on C++. However, the team could not get C++ to do everything they wanted in order to create a system to support a distributed network of communicating heterogeneous devices. The team abandoned C++ and developed a language called Oak (later renamed Java). By the fall of 1992, the team had created a project named Star 7 (*7), which was a personal, handheld remote control.

The development team was incorporated as FirstPerson, Inc., but then lost a bid to develop a television set-top box for Time-Warner. By the middle of 1994, the growth in the Web's popularity drew the team's attention. They decided they could build an excellent browser using Java technology. With a goal of bringing their CPU-independent, real-time programming system to the Web, they built a Web browser.

The browser, called WebRunner, was written using Java and completed early in the fall of 1994. Executives at Sun Microsystems were impressed and saw the technology and commercial possibilities that could result from a new browser: tools, servers, and development environments.

On May 23, 1995, Sun Microsystems, Inc., formally announced Java and HotJava at SunWorld '95 in San Francisco.

Java's Current Status and Timeline

For the most current information on Java's releases, see Sun Microsystem's Java site at `http://java.sun.com/`.

Java/HotJava timetable:

1. San Jose, California, April 11, 1995: Netscape chairman Jim Clark and Sun CEO Scott McNealy reaffirmed their working relationship and promised more news at SunWorld '95.

2. San Francisco, California, May 23, 1995: At SunWorld '95, Netscape announced that it will license Sun's Java programming language for its Netscape Navigator browser.

3. Summer 1995: Java and HotJava in alpha stages of development. Alpha release for Sun Solaris 2.3, 2.4, and 2.5 SPARC-based. Alpha release also for Microsoft Windows NT. Ports underway for Microsoft Windows 95 and MacOS 7.5. Ports are underway in third-party projects for other platforms and operating systems, including Windows 3.1, Amiga, NeXT, Silicon Graphics, and Linux.

4. Summer 1995: Sun Microsystems sponsored an applet programming contest to encourage the development of excellent applets. Winners will be announced on the HotJava home page (`http://java.sun.com/`) on September 15, 1995.

5. Expected Fall/Winter, 1995: Java technology to be integrated into Netscape browsers (see `http://home.netscape.com/`).

Java Future Possibilities

Java technology can be deployed in embedded systems—as in consumer electronics, such as handheld devices, telephones, and VCRs. Mitsubishi Electronics has been working to use Java technology in these devices.

The association of Netscape and Sun Microsystems should bring Java technology into Netscape browsers by late 1995. With Netscape's widespread installed base, the use of Java in applications could very rapidly increase.

Sun Microsystems also plans to license its Java technology to other Web browser manufacturers, online service providers, and software developers. The market for third-party object and tool libraries for Java is expected to take off. Software layers on top of Java will enable developers to use more sophisticated tools to create applications.

Illustrations of Java's Potential

Java is a new programming language, and programmers outside of Sun Microsystems are just beginning to explore its potential. However, you can see Java in action now. The rest of this chapter shows you examples of the basic kinds of activity Java can support, emphasizing the unique way Java enables the distribution of executable content. More details of applications in all areas of Java's potential are shown in Part II of this book.

Animation

Java's applications put animated figures on Web pages. Figure 1.3 shows a still image of Duke, the mascot of Java, who tumbles across a Web page displayed in the HotJava browser. Duke tumbles across the page, cycling through a set of graphic images that loop while the user has this page loaded in the HotJava browser.

Figure 1.3.
Tumbling Duke, mascot of Java. (Courtesy of Arthur van Hoff, Sun Microsystems)

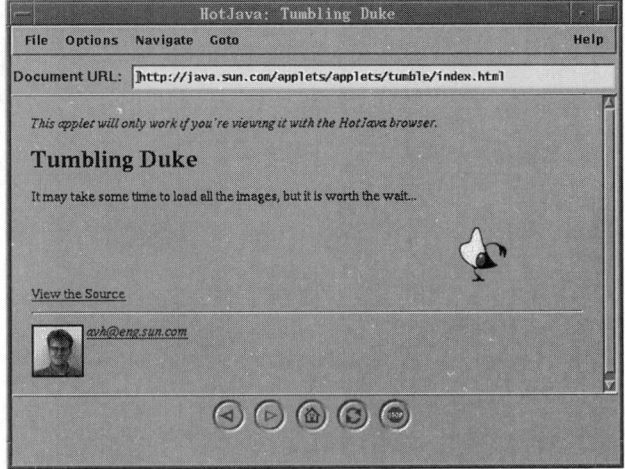

Animation isn't limited to cartoon figures, however. Pages can have animated logos or text that moves or shimmers across the screen. Java animations also need not just be a decorative pre-generated figure, but can be a graphic that is generated based on computation. Figure 1.4 shows a wave form drawn based on a mathematical equation.

Interaction

While the animations shown can be static images that are drawn or generated, or animated images that can behave according to a pre-set algorithm (such as the tumbling Duke in figure 1.3), animation can also be made interactive, where the user has some input on its appearance.

Figure 1.5 shows a three-dimensional rendering of chemical models. Using the mouse, you can spin these models and view them from many angles. Unlike the source code for the graph applet shown in figure 1.4, of course, the source code for the chemical modeling is more complicated. To the user, however, the chemical models seem three-dimensional, giving an insight into the nature of the atomic structure of these elements like no book could.

Figure 1.4.

A graph generated as a result of a mathematical formula. (Courtesy of Arthur van Hoff, Sun Microsystems)

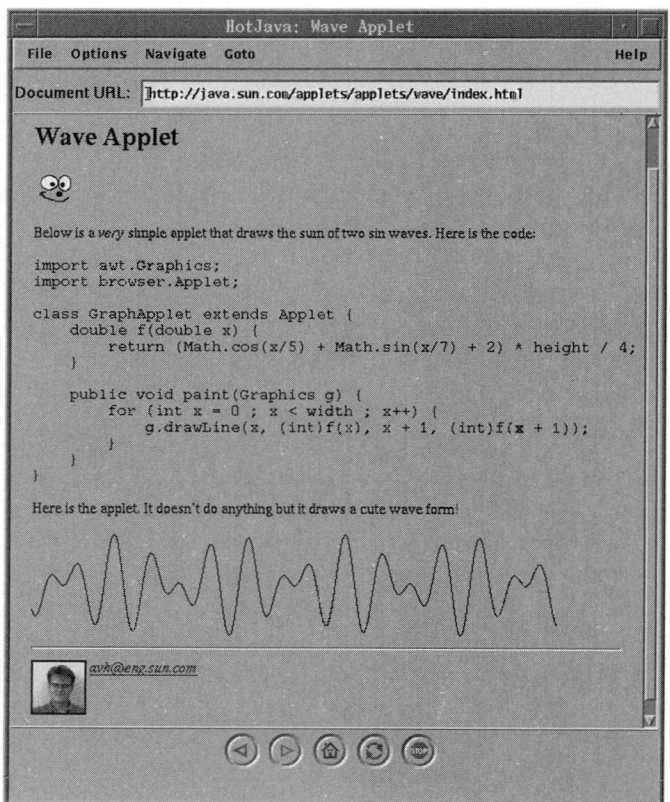

The chemical models in figure 1.5 respond to user clicks of the mouse. Another variation on this animation involves providing the user with a way to interact with an interface to enter data and get feedback. The crossword puzzle example in figure 1.6 is an excellent example of this. This application works just like a paper puzzle, except that the user enters guesses using the keyboard. Using the mouse to place the cursor in any square, a highlighted bar as well as the clue window at the top of the puzzle show the current word the user is guessing. Correct letters are displayed in black and incorrect letters are shown in red. In figure 1.6, 40 across is high-lighted, and the clue is shown in the window at the top. The letter "K" in 40 across is incorrect, as the letters of 26 down are in red (not distinguishable in the black and white image) to indi-cate an incorrect guess. This feedback gives the user an advantage for guessing that a paper crossword puzzle could not do. The resulting application is an excellent demonstration of how Java can create an interface for user interaction and immediate feedback.

Figure 1.5.
*Three-dimensional,
manipulatable chemical
models. (Courtesy of Sun
Microsystems)*

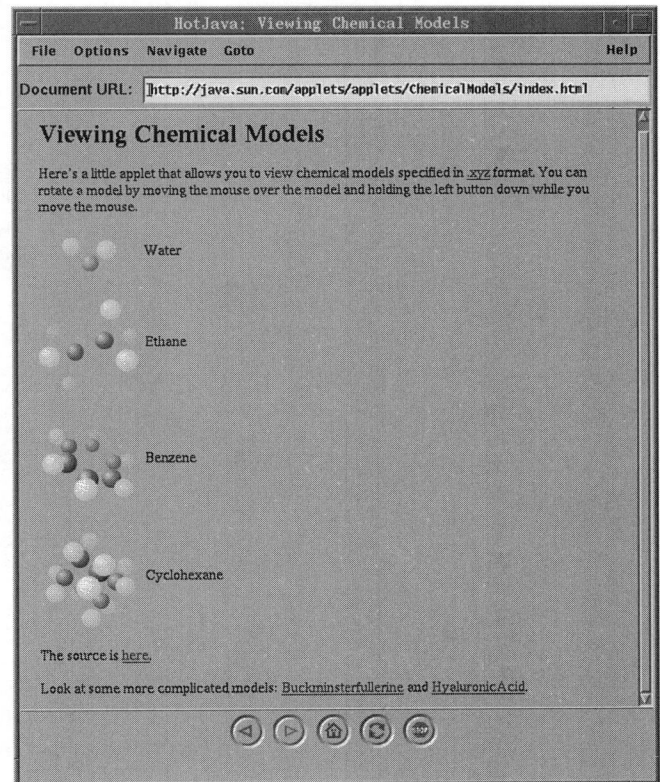

Another variation on interactivity is real-time interactivity. Figure 1.7 shows an inter-active application that involves moving graphics that the user manipulates. This is the game of Tetris, in which you can try to line up the falling tile shapes to completely fill the rectangle. Using designated keys for playing, you interact with the interface to steer the falling shapes. This Tetris implementation demonstrates the possibilities for arcade-like games using Java technology.

Figure 1.6.
*Interactive crossword
puzzle. (Courtesy of Carl
W. Haynes III)*

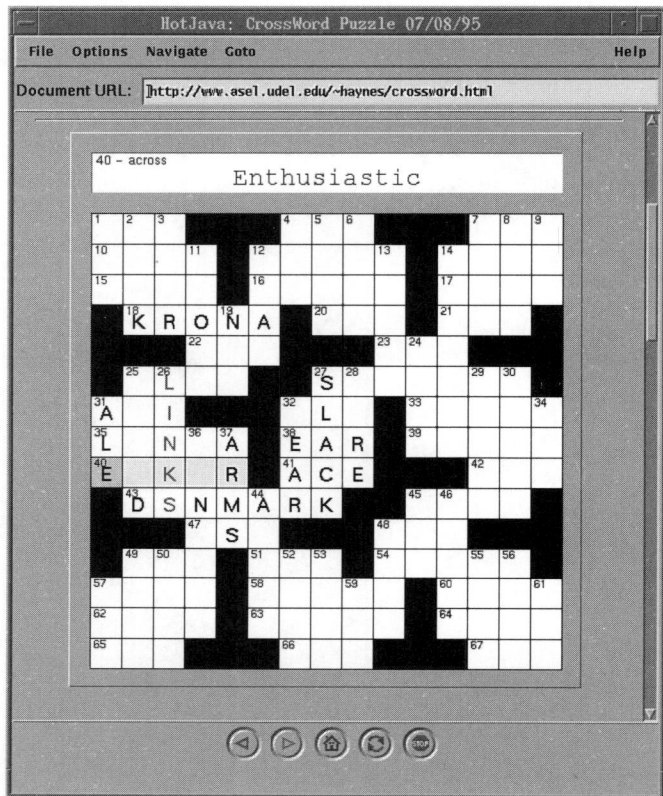

Interactivity and Computation

The crossword puzzle and Tetris game demonstrate how interactivity and animation can work together. Both applets customized their animated output based on user input, so both applets were actually performing computation. However, an example that shows this computational ability in more concrete terms is in figure 1.8, a simple spreadsheet.

This spreadsheet works in much the same manner as the crossword puzzle, but emphasizes that the computational possibilities can allow users to have an environment in which to work instead of just a puzzle to solve. The spreadsheet shown allows you to change the contents of any of the 24 cells (A1 through D6) by replacing its label, value, or formula. This is just like a real spreadsheet, which is more of an environment in which the user can work than a fixed game such as the crossword puzzle. This subtle difference is a profound one: using Java, a user can obtain an entire environment for open-ended interaction rather than a fixed set of options for interaction —opening up the Web page into a Web stage.

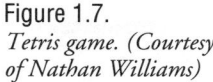

Figure 1.7.
Tetris game. (Courtesy of Nathan Williams)

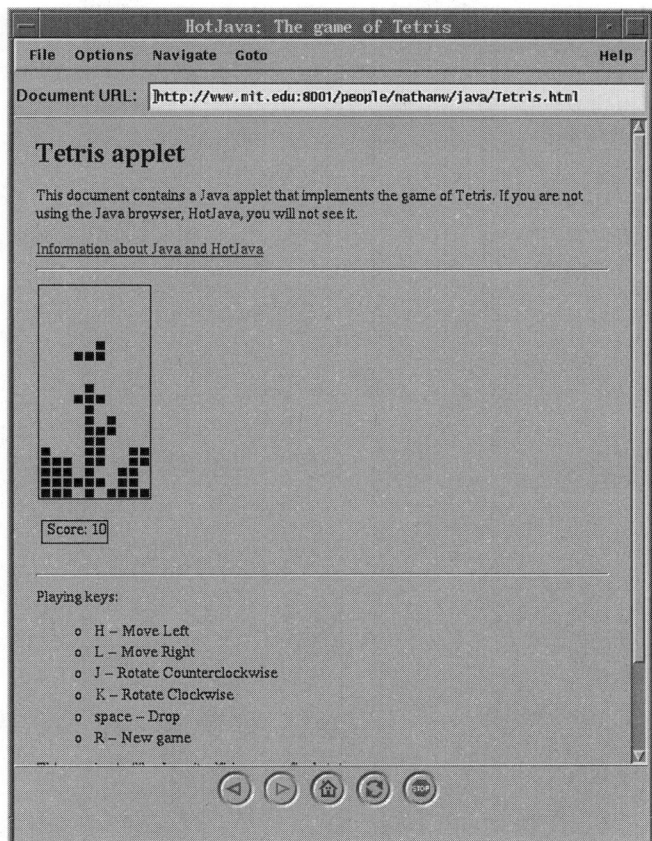

Distributed Applications

The oscilloscope shown in figure 1.9 operates in a HotJava browser and allows the user to manipulate its settings. The result is an application something like the chemical models but with continuous independent feedback to the user. Once the settings are made, the oscilloscope displays the figures that show the waveform of the electrical signals. This application shows animation, interaction, computation, and continuous display based on user settings. The result is that a user has essentially downloaded an oscilloscope remotely.

Just as the user can download an oscilloscope, so too can a user download a "kit" for doing almost anything. Figure 1.10 shows a makeover kit that demonstrates the possibilities with Java. This kit allows the user to select a color and a brush style and then paint on the face provided in the kit. This very simple paint application shows how the user can build something with a Java page.

Figure 1.8.
A simple spreadsheet.
(Courtesy of Sami Shaio,
Sun Microsystems)

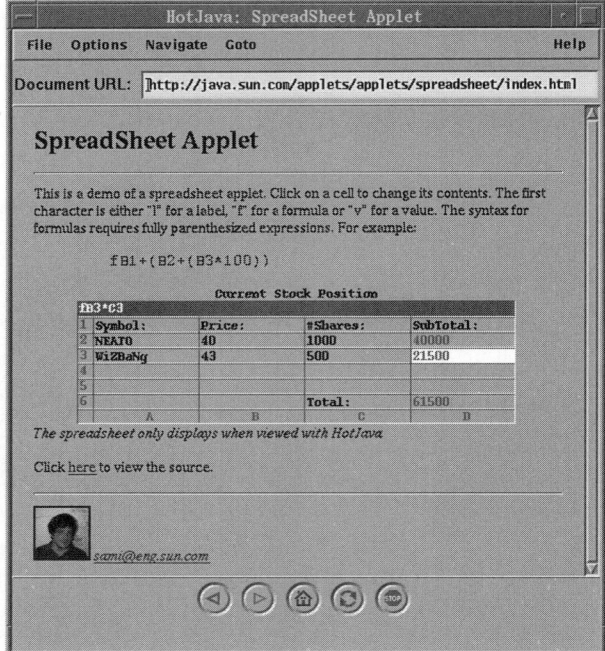

Figure 1.9.
An oscilloscope.
(Courtesy of Hugh
Anderson)

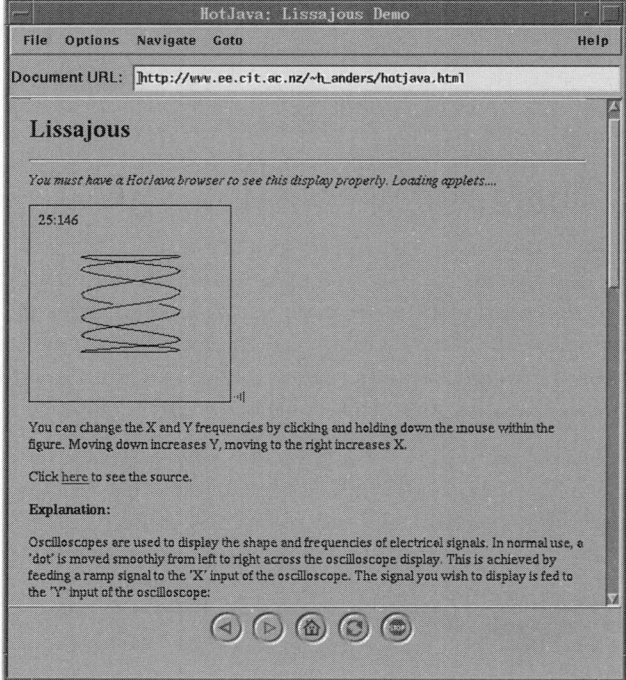

Figure 1.10.
A makeover kit.
(Courtesy of George
Coates Performance
Works)

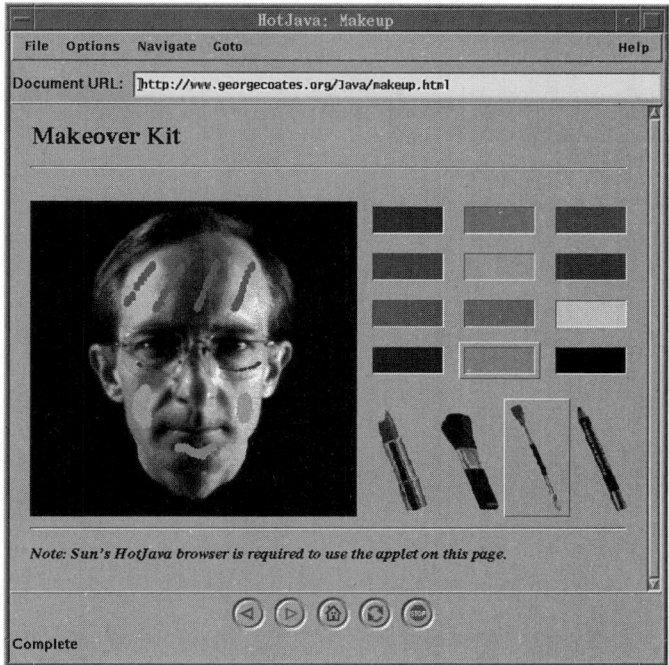

Communication

The preceding examples demonstrate many informational, animation, and computational applications of Java. Another application area is communication among people. Carl W. Haynes III has implemented a simple Java-based chat system, shown in figure 1.11. This system allows you to log in to this Web page and type sentences that are seen by others who are viewing that page. The text you type is visible to all others who have the page displayed in their Java-enabled browsers. This results in a group chat system similar to that implemented in a Telnet, Internet Relay Chat, or MU* systems.

Of course, communication takes place all the time on nearly all Web pages through text or other media. But a Java-enabled browser can also display multimedia. Figure 1.12 illustrates a simple speaking clock—you can retrieve the current time as sound in response to a mouse click on the clock display.

Java can also be used to support mass communication in new ways. The NandO Times is a Web-based news service that has been very innovative in news delivery on the Web. Using Java, this news agency now provides a tickertape of headlines across its front page. The text under the NandO banner in figure 1.13 scrolls continuously to show the top world, national, sports, and political stories at the moment. The four pictures under the labels for these categories also change, giving a "slide show" that is very effective in displaying new information without requiring the user to select it for viewing. This transforms the Web into something people can watch to get new information.

Figure 1.11.
*A Java-based chat
system. (Courtesy of Carl
W. Haynes III)*

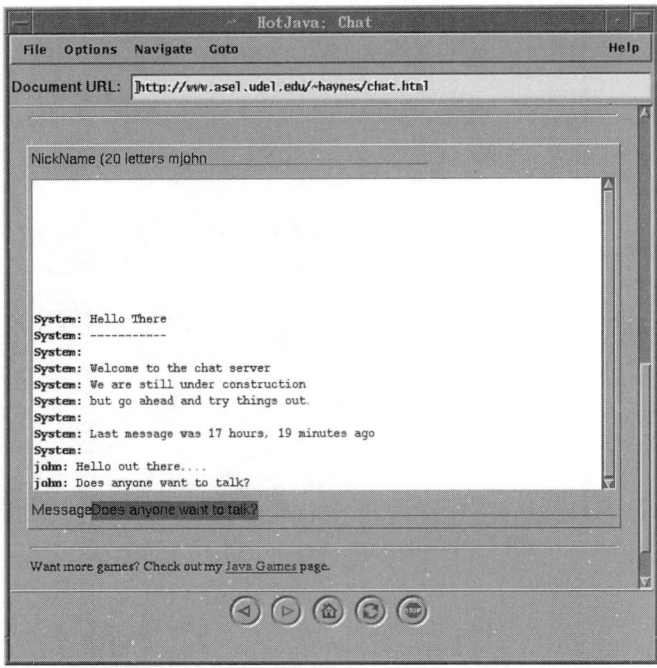

Figure 1.12.
*A speaking clock.
(Courtesy of Arthur van
Hoff, Sun Microsystems)*

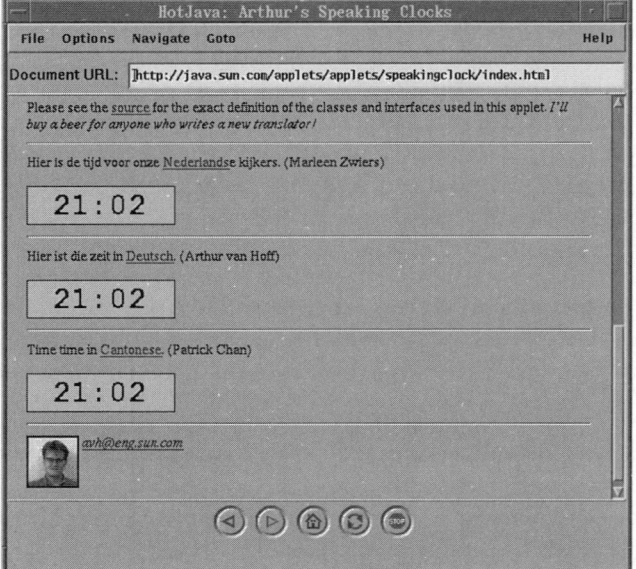

Figure 1.13.
Headline feed on
NandO Times.
(Courtesy of NandO
Times)

Similarly, figure 1.14 shows how current information feeds can act as surveillance for specific activities. The figure shows a test of ESPNET's SportsZone Live Scoreboard, showing the current scores of games in progress. As the scores change, this display changes, so that the sports-minded can keep up with the current games and scores. Like the *NandO Times* news feed, this sports feed changes the Web into something to watch in addition to something to interact with.

Applications and Handlers

In addition to applets like the ones shown here, Java programmers can also create applications, or standalone programs, that don't require the Java-enabled browser to run. (The HotJava browser itself is such an application, written using Java.) Applications could thus conceivably be new browsers or interfaces that interact with other network or local resources.

Another kind of software program available with Java is a *handler*. A protocol handler enables a Java programmer to specify how a Java browser should interpret a particular type of protocol. The HotJava browser knows how to interpret the Internet protocols such as HTTP, FTP, Gopher, and others because of the browser distribution code. But if new protocols are invented, a Java programmer can specify how they should be handled by creating a protocol handler.

Figure 1.14.
ESPNET SportsZone Live Scoreboard. (Courtesy of Jonathan Payne, Starwave Corporation)

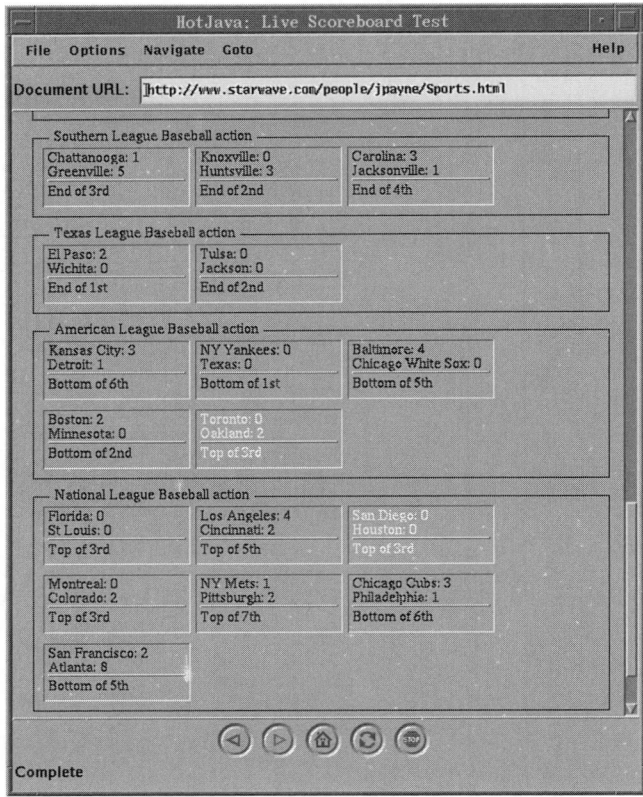

Another type of handler is a content handler. This handler translates a particular specification for a file type based on Multipurpose Internet Mail Extensions (MIME). This content handler will specify how the HotJava browser should handle a particular type of file type. By creating a specification in a content handler, all Java-enabled browsers will be able to view this special format.

The handlers and applications that Java makes possible have the potential to dramatically extend what can be browsed on the Web. No longer will information developers have to be concerned about making sure their users have the proper software to view a particular type of file or handle a new kind of protocol. The protocol and content handlers, like the executable content Java makes possible as applets, can be distributed as needed to requesting Java-enabled browsers.

What Java Might Make Possible

The previous examples illustrate only some of the potential of Java. A few of these examples are "toy" demonstrations meant to show the possibilities of Java. What kind of communication might Java foster? The *NandO Times* example shows an innovative application for providing information in a way that allows you to sit back and observe rather than selecting hypertext links.

Java opens up a new degree of interactivity and customizability of interaction for the Web. Earlier Web development techniques of creating pages and linking them together will still be necessary in a Java-flavored Web. However, Java creates possibilities for richer kinds of content to be developed. The user can interact with and change the appearance of a Web page along with the state of a database using a Java-enabled browser. Thus, Java profoundly changes the texture of the Web in the following ways:

- **Java creates places to stop on the paths of the Web.** A well-done Java application on a single hypertext page can engage a user for a long time. Rather than just text, sound, images, or videos to observe, a Java page can offer a place to play, learn, or communicate and interact with others in a way that isn't necessarily based on going somewhere else on the Web through hyperlinks. If the hypertext of the Web are like paths, the Java pages are like the towns, villages, and cities to stop on these paths and do something other than just observe or "surf."

- **Java increases the dynamism and competitiveness of the Web.** Just as new browser technology prompted Web developers to create still more applications and pages to exploit these features, so too does Java technology promise a new round of content development on the Web.

- **Java enriches the interactivity of the Web.** Java's interactivity is far richer, more immediate, and more transparent than the interactivity possible through gateway programming. Gateway programming still should have a role in Web applications, just as page design and multimedia presentation will still play a role. However, Java's interactivity brings new possibilities of what can happen on the Web. With Java, transactions on the Web can be more customized, with immediate, continuous, and ongoing feedback to the user.

- **Java transforms the Web into a software delivery system.** Java's essential design as a language to deliver executable content makes it possible for programmers to create software of any kind and deliver it to users of HotJava browsers. Rather than having to focus on the interface, the Java programmer focuses on the interaction desired and lets the built-in features of the graphics take care of the rest of the implementation. The result is that very simple programs like the drawing and spreadsheet applications can be created quickly and distributed worldwide.

The true potential of Java to transform the Web is still in its initial stages. New potential applications for commerce, information delivery, and user interaction still await the imagination and skill of future Java developers.

Chapter Summary

Java is a programming language designed to deliver executable content over networks. A user or programmer should know what kinds of interaction Java can make possible and what its true potential can be: enlivening the Web, enriching the display of information in the form of animation and interactive applications.

- Java enriches the interactivity possible on the Web. Rather than making just informational content possible, Java can support interactive content in the form of software that can be downloaded and run on any computer host with the Java interpretation environment installed.

- Java was developed from ideas about platform-independent executable code. Sun Microsystems researchers have developed Java to be a powerful programming and information delivery system for use with the Web.

- Java makes animation, interaction, computation, distributed applications, and new forms of communication possible. Through protocol and content handlers, Java has the potential to make new formats and new protocols available for use on the Web.

- Java transforms the Web into a software delivery system where users have things to do rather than just places to go. Java may change the surfing behavior of Web users into playing and learning behavior in new interactive environments.

Java's Design Is Flexible and Dynamic

The Java programming language is technically unique. It offers a set of characteristics tailored to its role for delivering executable content across networks, as well as an extensible set of features for programmers. This chapter presents an overview of the technical design of Java. I begin with a minimal example of a "hello world" Java program. This should prepare you to understand how Java and HTML connect. Using this information, you can then try out some of the Java programs shown in Part II of this book.

Java also has specialized characteristics. In the second part of this chapter, I discuss in more technical detail how Java supports executable, distributed applications.

A Hello to Java

The first part of understanding the technical details of Java is learning how Java interacts with the Web's hypertext. The example shown in this section demonstrates how a special tag of the hypertext markup language (HTML) associates a Java program called an applet to a page on the Web. Viewed through a Java-enabled Web browser, a page with a Java applet can come alive with animation or interaction.

Java's Connection to the Web

As a language for delivering information on the Web, Java connects to the Web's hypertext markup language (HTML) using a special tag called APP. Figure 2.1 summarizes this connection: a document on a Web server written in HTML is downloaded to the user's browser by request. Through the APP tag, this document identifies the Java code of the applet. If the user's Web browser is Java-enabled, the applet runs in the user's browser.

Figure 2.1.
Java's connection to the Web through the APP *tag.*

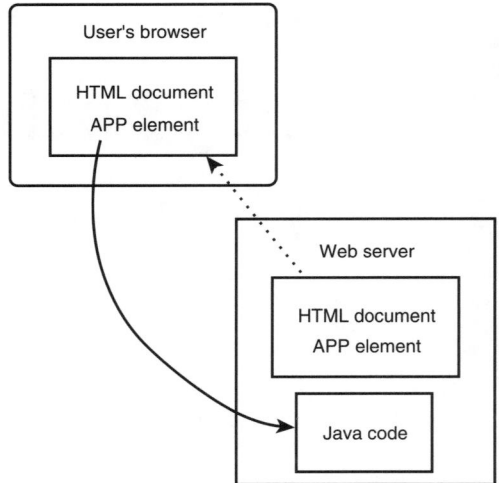

A technical understanding of Java also requires a familiarity with HTML. HTML is the markup language used to create the documents displayed in Web browsers. HTML is not a layout language for describing how a page of hypertext should look (although there are many features of HTML that can be used to manipulate a page's appearance). Rather, HTML tags the structure of a document and the meaning of text so that a browser can display it in a scheme based on that browser's design and the user's preferences for the font size, style, and other features.

An HTML document consists of text and tags that mark the structure of the document. Tags in an HTML document are delimited by the brackets < and >. Some tags always appear in a pair, as a start and end tag. For example, you can identify the title of an HTML document by placing the tags <TITLE> and </TITLE> around the text of the document's title. Other tags don't require a corresponding ending tag. For example, you can identify a paragraph using the <P> tag.

Some tags have *attributes*, which qualify the tag's meaning.

Here is a simple HTML document:

```
<HTML>
<HEAD>
   <TITLE>Example HTML Document</TITLE>
</HEAD>
<BODY>
   <P>
   This is the body of the document.
   <OL>
   <LI>This is the first item in an ordered list.
   <LI>This is the second item.
   <OL>
</BODY>
</HTML>
```

When a Web browser interprets these HTML tags and text, it displays it without the brackets < and >. A text-only browser renders this simple HTML example as:

```
Example HTML Document
This is the body of the document.
   1. This is the first item in an ordered list.
   2. This is the second item.
```

Appendix C contains more HTML tags presented in a reference table, showing many more features of HTML that are available. Note that the only Java-enabled browser at the time of this writing, HotJava, does not recognize all levels of HTML or extensions to HTML. The simple HTML example shown here should be enough to get you started in understanding how HTML connects to Java.

A Simple Java Program

The APP tag in an HTML document identifies the name of a Java program called an applet to be included in a Web page. The name of the applet is called its *class name*. This name is associated with the executable bytecodes that run the applet.

For example, the following HTML example demonstrates how you can include an applet in a Web document. If you want to test this, put the following lines in a file called HelloWorld.html:

```
<HTML>
<HEAD>
   <TITLE>First Hello Applet</TITLE>
</HEAD>
<BODY>
   <P>"This is it!" <APP Class="HelloWorld">
</BODY>
</HTML>
```

Of course, you need to create the Java source code for the applet named HelloWorld. You can find more details on programming in Java in Part IV of this book. For now, here is a minimal Java applet as a simple demonstration:

```
/*
   This is the first hello.
*/

import browser.Applet;
import awt.Graphics;

class HelloWorld extends Applet {
   public void init() {
      resize(600, 300);
   }
   public void paint(Graphics g) {
      g.drawString("Hello world!", 50, 100);
   }
}
```

Alpha Release of Java

This Java source code example as well as others in this book were compiled using the *alpha* release of Java. For updates on these source code examples for *beta* and later releases of Java, see this book's support web at http://www.rpi.edu/~decemj/works/java.html.

You can place Java code in a file named HelloWorld.java. Next, you have to compile the Java source file using the Java compiler. At the operating system prompt ($), enter:

```
$ javac HelloWorld.java
```

If there are no compilation errors, the compiler will create a file named HelloWorld.class that contains the bytecodes for the HelloWorld applet. Place this HelloWorld.class file in a subdirectory named classes.

So at this point, you have:

- A file called HelloWorld.html.
- A file called HelloWorld.java.
- A file called HelloWorld.class that is in a subdirectory called classes. This is a subdirectory relative to the directory containing the file HelloWorld.java. Figure 2.2 summarizes the Java source code and compilation relationships.

If you start a Java-enabled browser (see Part III of this book for how to obtain the HotJava browser), you can test this applet. Use the browser to open the file HelloWorld.html. Figure 2.3 shows what this example looks like in a HotJava browser.

Figure 2.2.
Java source code and compilation relationships.

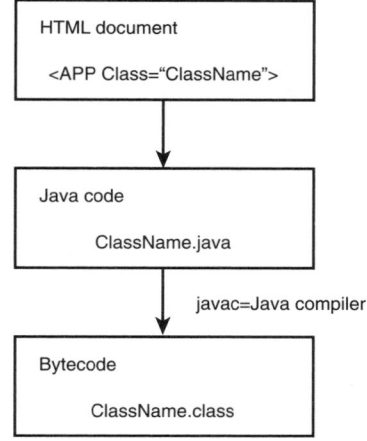

Figure 2.3.
Java Browser display of the HelloWorld applet.

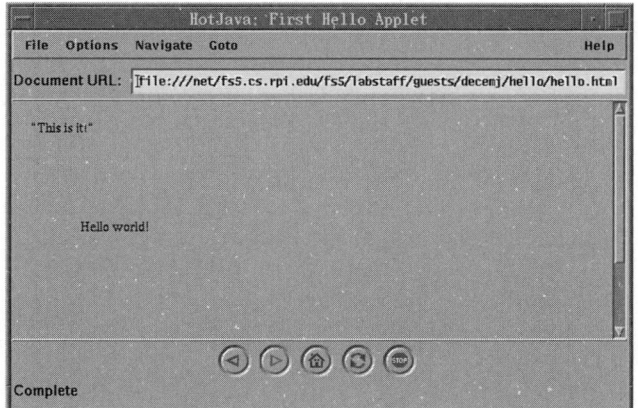

Java Technical Overview

The preceding example concretely demonstrates the connection of Java applets to the Web through the APP tag. But this is only a view of Java from a very beginning perspective. To help you understand Java's design and potential, this section provides a technical overview of the language.

Java is an object-oriented programming language that is used in conjunction with Java-enabled Web browsers. These browsers can interpret the bytecodes created by the Java language compiler. The technical design of Java is *architecture neutral.* The term *architecture* in this sense refers to computer hardware. For example, your computer's architecture could be an IBM personal computer with an Intel 386 chip. Programmers can create Java programs without having to worry about the underlying architecture of a user's computer. Instead, the HotJava browser is customized to the user's architecture. The HotJava browser interprets the bytecodes for the particular architecture of the user. This is a key characteristic of Java's technical design.

The Network Communication Support Ring Around Java

Before delving into Java's technical characteristics, it might help to step back and look at the "big picture" of how Java fits into the Web and online communication.

This entire operation of Java and Java-enabled browsers on the Web takes place in a larger context of online communication, requiring the interoperation of a variety of network systems. You don't have to understand the inter-operation of all of these systems to use HotJava. (You can go directly to Part III to find out what you need to obtain HotJava.) But, stepping back a bit from what Java is, we can look at its context, in terms of a "support ring" of networks and applications.

The goal of Java is to bring executable content to the Web. When installed, a Java-enabled browser can provide an interface to animated and interactive applications. To view and interact with these applications, you must have a computer with a Java-capable browser installed. If you want to download content from all over the Web, you also must have an Internet connection.

Beginning with the widest context for the operation of the Java technology, let's take a look at the systems necessary to support Java when delivering information globally (again, Java can be used on local networks not requiring the Internet):

1. Cyberspace is the mental model people have for communicating or interacting online or through computers. Cyberspace activity includes a variety of information, communication, and interaction for users. Cyberspace can be thought of as consisting of non-networked and networked regions. The networked region in cyberspace includes activity on connected local, regional, and global computer networks.

2. The Internet computer network serves as a vehicle for data communication for many information dissemination protocols. Through gateways, many other networks in cyberspace can exchange data with the Internet. Because of this and also because of the large amount of information available on the Internet, it serves as a common ground for the networked region of cyberspace.

3. The Web is an application that relies on a client/server model for data communication. While the Web can operate on local networks that have no connection to the Internet, the Web is popularly known for its collection of information that is available globally through the Internet.

4. A Web client, known as a browser, is a software program that interprets and displays information disseminated using a variety of Internet information protocols. A Web browser is a user's interface into the Web and operates in conjunction with a variety of helper applications to display multimedia.

5. HTML is used to create hypertext for the Web and marks the semantic structure of Web documents. HTML consists of tags and entities that identify the structure and meaning of text in documents.

6. The APP tag associates Java applications with HTML documents. This tag occurs in an HTML document and identifies a Java applet that will be placed in that document.

7. A Java-enabled browser dowloads hypertext as well as the executable bytecodes of the applet. The browser interprets and displays the applet, allowing a user to view or interact with the applet.

Figure 2.4 summarizes the support rings for Java as it is used for worldwide distribution of information.

Figure 2.4.
The support rings of
systems around Java.

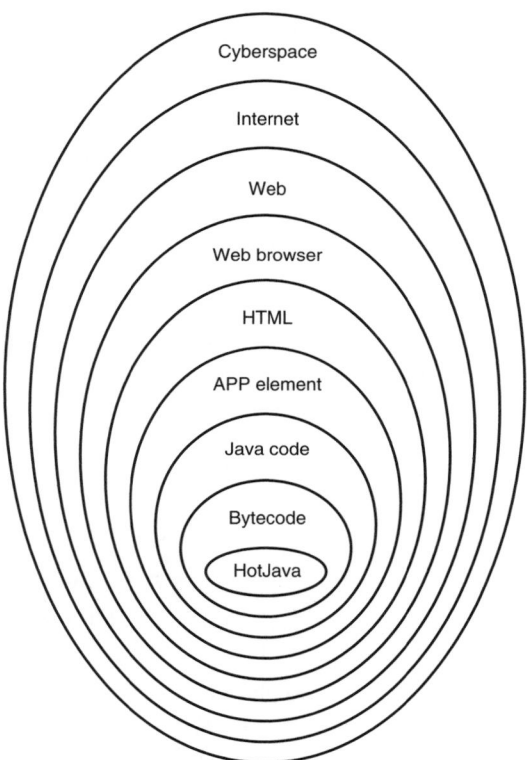

Again, you don't have to know how to set up the entire range of networks, software, and equipment in Java's "support rings." All you need is to install a Java-enabled browser on your Internet-accessible system. From your point of view as a user, your main focus is your browser. Figure 2.4 summarizes the other systems to help your awareness of the context in which this communication occurs. You can use this awareness to help place yourself within larger communication contexts.

Characteristics of Java as a Programming Language

While users may want to have some awareness of how Java fits into online communication, programmers may want to understand the technical characteristics of Java. The description in this section introduces many terms for a programmer audience.

According to the information provided by Sun Microsystems (http://java.sun.com/), Java is

> [a] simple, object-oriented, distributed, interpreted, robust, secure, architecture-neutral, portable, high-performance, multithreaded, and dynamic language.

This characterization identifies the key technical features of Java:

simple   The developers of Java based it on the C++ programming language, but removed many of the object-oriented features that are rarely used or often used poorly. C++ is a language for object-oriented programming and offers very powerful features. However, as is the case with many languages designed to have power, some features often cause programmers problems, such as creating code that often contains errors and is poorly understood. Because the majority of the cost of software engineering is often code maintenance rather than creation, this shift to understandable code rather than powerful but poorly understood code can help reduce software costs. Specifically, Java differs from C++ (and C) in these ways:

1. Java does not support the struct, union, and pointer data types.
2. Java does not support typedef or #define.
3. Java differs in its handling of certain operators and does not permit operator overloading.
4. Java does not support multiple inheritance.
5. Java handles command line arguments differently than C or C++.
6. Java has a String class as part of the java.lang package. This differs from the null-terminated array of characters as used in C and C++.
7. Java has an automatic system for allocating and freeing memory (garbage collection), so it is unnecessary to use memory allocation and de-allocation functions as in C and C++.

object-oriented   Like C++, Java can support an object-oriented approach to writing software. Ideally, object-oriented design can permit the creation of software components that can be re-used.

Object-oriented programming is based upon modeling the world in terms of software components called *objects*. An object consists of data and operations called *methods* that can be performed on that data. These methods encapsulate, or protect, an object's data because the methods are the only way to change the state of the data.

Another aspect of object-orientation is *inheritance.* Objects can use characteristics of other objects without having to reproduce the functionality of those objects. Inheritance thus helps in software re-use. Another benefit of inheritance is software organization. Having objects organized according to classes means that each object in a class inherits characteristics from parent objects. This makes the job of documenting, understanding, and benefiting from previous generations of software easier, because the functionality of the software is incrementally grown as more objects are created. Objects at the end of a long inheritance chain can be very specialized and powerful. Figure 2.5 summarizes the general qualities of data encapsulation, methods, and inheritance of an object-oriented language.

Figure 2.5.
Object-orientation in
software.

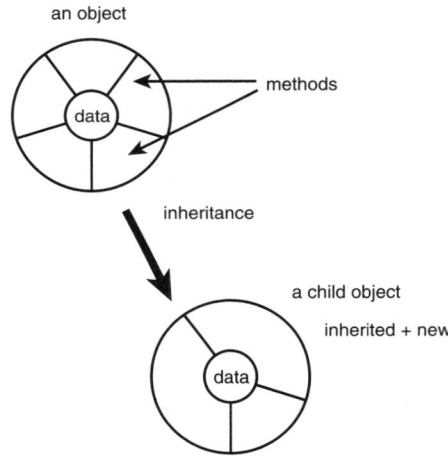

Technically, Java's object-oriented features are those of C++ with extensions from Objective C for dynamic method resolution.

distributed	Unlike the languages C++ and C, Java is specifically designed to work within a networked environment. Java has a large library of classes for communicating using the Internet's TCP/IP protocol suite, including protocols such as HTTP and FTP. Java code can manipulate resources via URLs as easily as programmers are used to accessing a local file system using C or C++.
interpreted	When the Java compiler translates a Java class source file to bytecodes, this bytecode class file can be run on any machine that runs a Java-enabled browser. This allows the Java code to be written independent of platform, and it eliminates the compile and run cycle for the client because the bytecodes are not specific to a given machine but interpreted.

robust

Robust software doesn't "break" easily because of programming bugs in it. A programming language that encourages robust software often places more restrictions on the programmer when he or she is writing the source code. These restrictions include those on data types and the user of pointers. The C programming language is notoriously lax in its checking of compatible data types during compilation and runtime. C++ was designed to be more strongly typed; however, C++ retains some of C's lax approach toward typing. In Java, typing is more rigorous: a programmer cannot turn an arbitrary integer into a pointer by casting, for example. Also, Java does not support pointer arithmetic but has arrays instead. This simplification eliminates some of the tricks that C programmers could use to access arbitrary areas of memory. In particular, Java does not allow the programmer to overwrite memory and corrupt other data through pointers. In contrast, a C programmer often can accidentally (or deliberately) overwrite or corrupt data.

secure

Because Java works in networked environments, the issue of security is one that should be of concern to developers. Plans are in the works for Java to use public-key encryption techniques to authenticate data. Java's limits on pointers won't allow developers to forge access to memory where they are not permitted. These aspects of Java enable a more secure software environment. The last section of this chapter outlines the layers of Java's security.

architecture-neutral

The Java compiler creates bytecode that is sent to the requesting browser and interpreted on that machine, which has the Java interpreter or a Java-enabled browser installed.

portable

The quality of being architecture neutral allows for a great deal of portability. However, another aspect of portability is how the hardware interprets arithmetic operations. In C and C++, source code may run slightly differently on different hardware platforms because of how these platforms implement arithmetic operations. In Java, this has been simplified. An integer type in Java, int, is a signed two's complement 32-bit integer. A real number, float, is always a 32-bit floating point number defined by the IEEE 754 standard.

high-performance	Because Java bytecodes are interpreted, the performance sometimes isn't as fast as direct compilation and execution on a particular hardware platform. Java compilation includes an option to translate the bytecodes into machine code for the particular hardware platform. This can give the same efficiency as a traditional compile and load process. According to Sun Microsystems testing, performance of this bytecode to machine code translation is "almost indistinguishable" from direct compilation from C or C++ programs.
multithreaded	Java is a language that can be used to create applications in which several things happen at once. Based on a system of routines that allow for multiple "threads" of events based on C. A. R. Hoare's monitor and condition paradigm, Java presents the programmer with a way to support real-time, interactive behavior in programs.
dynamic	Unlike C++ code, which often requires complete recompilation if a parent class is changed, Java uses a method of interfaces to relieve this dependency. The result is that Java programs can allow for new methods and instance variables in a library of objects without affecting their dependent client objects.

Java in Operation

Another way to understand the technical description of Java is to look at the processes that occur when a user with a Java-enabled browser requests a page containing a Java applet. Figure 2.6 shows this process:

1. The user sends a request for an HTML document to the information provider's server.

2. The HTML document is returned to the user's browser. The document contains the APP tag, which identifies the applet.

3. The corresponding applet bytecode is transferred to the user's host. This bytecode had been previously created by the Java compiler using the Java source code file for that applet.

4. The Java-enabled browser on the user's host interprets the bytecodes and provides the display.

5. The user may have further interaction with the applet but with no further downloading from the provider's Web server. This is because the bytecode contains all the information necessary to interpret the applet.

Figure 2.6.
*Java operation within a
Web page.*

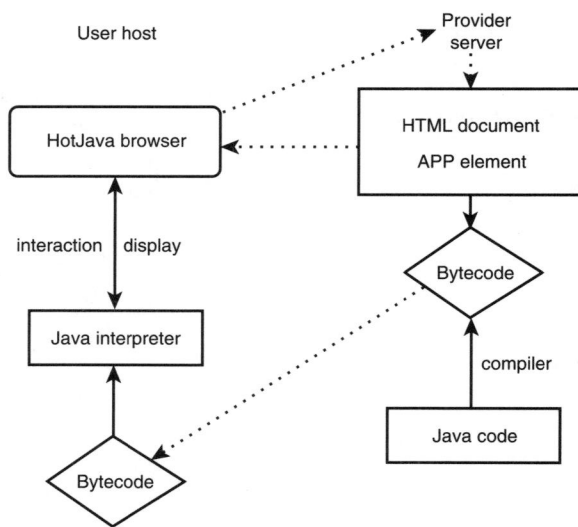

Java Software Components

Another aspect of the technical make-up of the Java environment is the software components that comprise its environment.

Java Language Constructs

Java is the programming language used to develop executable, distributed applications for delivery to a HotJava browser or the Java Interpreter. A Java programmer can create:

- **applets**: Programs that are included in HTML pages through the APP tag and displayed in the HotJava browser. The simple "hello world" program shown at the start of this chapter is an applet. The HotJava browser is invoked by the hotjava command included in the Java code distribution.

- **applications**: Stand-alone programs written in Java and executed independently of the HotJava browser. This is done using the Java interpreter, java, included in the Java code distribution.

- **protocol handlers**: Programs that are loaded into the user's HotJava browser and interpret a protocol. These protocols include standard ones such as HTTP or programmer-defined protocols.

- **content handlers**: A program loaded into the user's HotJava browser, which interprets files of a type defined by the Java programmer. The Java programmer provides the necessary code for the user's HotJava browser to display/interpret this special format.

■ **native methods**: Methods that are declared in a Java class but implemented in C. These native methods essentially allow a Java programmer to access C code from Java.

Java Distribution Software

The Java code distribution includes the following pieces:

■ **HotJava**: This is the World Wide Web browser used to view and interact with Java programs. It is invoked with the hotjava command provided with the Java code distribution.

■ **Java interpreter**: This is the Java interpreter that can be ported to a variety of hardware platforms. This interpreter or a Java-enabled browser must be installed and operating on the user's system in order for the user to observe Java content. The size of this basic interpreter and basic class support is around 40 KB bytes (alpha release). Standard libraries and thread support raise this an additional 175 KB. This relatively small size makes Java very portable. The interpreter is invoked with the java command.

■ **Java compiler**: This is the software used to translate the human-readable Java source code to machine-readable bytecodes. The Java compiler is invoked using the javac command.

■ **C header and source file generator**: Generates C header and source files for making methods. Invoked with the javah or javah_g command.

■ **Java disassembler**: Prints out information about a class file (a file created using the Java compiler). Invoked with the javap command.

■ **Document generator**: This can generate a page of documentation given a source file. It is invoked with the javadoc command. For example, figure 2.7 shows the results of javadoc operation on the HelloWorld class.

■ **Profiling tool**: This formats the output of the -prof option of the Java interpreter, java. Invoked with the javaprof command.

■ **Documentation:** The Java distribution also includes a wealth of documentation. You can access this documentation using the built-in features of the HotJava browser. (See Part III, "Using the HotJava Browser.")

Figure 2.7.
*Java Document
generation from the
HelloWorld class.*

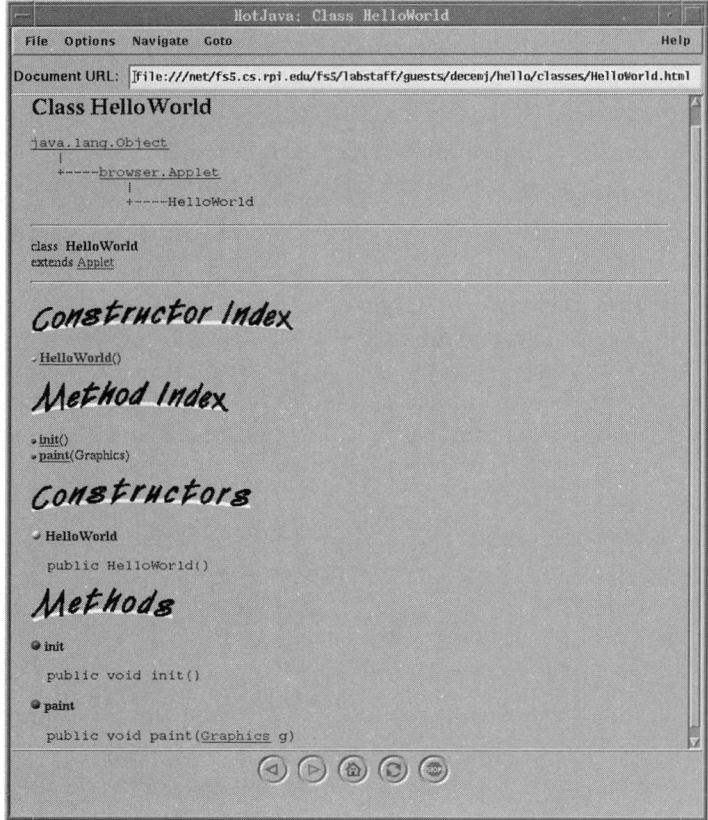

The Java Application Programming Interface

The Java Application Programming Interface (API) is a set of classes that are distributed with the Java source code and which programmers can use in Java applications. The documentation of the API that is provided online is key reference material for Java programmers. The API consists of the packages in the Java language. The API documentation includes a list of

- All packages
- All classes in a package
- A selected class

Java packages include:

- package `java.lang`: Language features such as object, thread, exception, character, integer, and string.
- package `java.util`: Utility features such as cache, linker, stack, and vector.

- **package** `java.io`: Input/Output features such as output stream, print stream, and text input stream. Java programmers can use these packages and classes to create more functionality. Part IV of this book goes into detail about programming in Java.

The Java Virtual Machine Specification

A document available from the Sun Microsystems Java site (`http://java.sun.com/`) called The Java Virtual Machine, specifies how the Java language is designed to exchange executable content across networks. The aim of this specification is to describe Java as a nonproprietary, open language that may be implemented by many companies and sold as a package.

The Java Virtual Machine specification describes in abstract terms how Java operates. This leaves the details of implementation up to the programmers who create Java interpreters and compilers. The Java Virtual Machine specification also concretely defines the specific interchange format for Java code. This is called The Java Interchange Specification.

The other part of the Virtual Machine specification defines the abstractions that can be left to the implementor. These abstractions are not related to the interchange of Java code. These include, for example, management of runtime data areas, garbage collection algorithms, the implementation of the compiler and other Java environment software, and optimization algorithms on compiled Java code.

Java Security

Because a HotJava browser downloads code across the network and then executes it on the user's host, security is a major concern for HotJava users and Java programmers.

HotJava includes several layers of security, including the following:

- The Java language itself includes tight restrictions on memory access very different from the memory model used in the C language. These restrictions include removal of pointer arithmetic and removal of illegal cast operators.
- A bytecode verification routine in the Java interpreter verifies that bytecodes don't violate any language constructs (which might happen if an altered Java compiler were used). This verification routine checks to make sure the code doesn't forge pointers, access restricted memory, or access objects other than according to their definitions. This check also ensures that method calls include the correct number of arguments of the right type, and that there are no stack overflows.
- A verification of class name and access restrictions during loading.
- An interface security system that enforces security policies at many levels.
- At the file access level, if a bytecode attempts to access a file to which it has no permissions, a dialog box will pop up allowing the user to continue or stop the execution.

- At the network level, future releases will have facilities to use public key encryption and other cryptographic techniques to verify the source of the code and its integrity after having passed through the network. This encryption technology will be the key to secure financial transactions across the network.

- At runtime, information about the origin of the bytecode can be used to decide what that code can do. The security mechanism can tell if a bytecode originated from inside a firewall or not. You can set a security policy that restricts code that you don't trust.

Chapter Summary

The Java programming language is uniquely designed to deliver executable content across networks. As a language, it flexibly offers features for programmers to create a variety of software. Java also assures interoperability among platforms as well as security.

- The Java programming language works in conjunction with a special kind of browser and bytecode interpreter. Java can exist within the context of World Wide Web communication and therefore "sits on top of" a large amount of applications on networks for data communications to support information retrieval.

- The Java language is object-oriented and specially designed to support distributed, executable applications.

- In operation, the Java language compiler creates bytecodes that are downloaded across the network to a user's computer. The user's computer runs these bytecodes.

- Components of Java software include the HotJava browser, the Java interpreter, the Java compiler, and tools for developing Java applications.

- Java's designs for security are tailored for distributing executable content on networks.

Java Transforms the World Wide Web

The World Wide Web has dramatically changed the online world and continues to grow in popularity. As a communication system, the Web can give information providers the ability to distribute and collect information globally and instantly. For users, the Web is a dynamic view into the works and ideas of millions of people and organizations worldwide. With origins in ideas about non-linear thinking, the Web is an information integrator on the Internet and plays a major role in cyberspace.

What Java brings to the Web is a new way of communicating. Instead of relying on the Web servers to provide information and functionality, Java's executable content makes Java-enabled Web browsers "smart."

This chapter briefly explores how Java transforms the World Wide Web. The Web supports a range of communication, information, and interaction using hypertext for organizing information. Multimedia used with hypertext, called *hypermedia*, can enrich the Web's information. Special programming techniques used with the Web's hypertext, such as gateway programming or languages such as Java or Virtual Reality Modeling Language, can expand the Web's possibilities for interactivity, information delivery, and communication.

To learn Java's power as it can be used for the global distribution of information, you should first understand what the Web is and the significance of Java's changes to it. If you are a seasoned Web user, you probably have already realized from the previous two chapters how Java extends the Web's potential; you might want to skip to Chapter 4 to begin looking at specifics. This chapter takes a close look at the Web and Java's part in it.

Overview of the Web

The World Wide Web was originally developed to meet the information needs of researchers in the high energy physics community. Today, the World Wide Web offers a system for distributing hypermedia information locally or globally. Technically, the World Wide Web enables a seamless, global system of multimedia communication. This information is organized associatively and delivered according to user requests. This section briefly surveys the historical origins of the Web and how the confluence of ideas in network technology has reached fruition in the global Web of today. Java is just the latest installment of a series of innovations in hypertext and Web communication.

Ideas Leading to the Web

Vannevar Bush described a system for associatively linking information in his July 1945 article in *The Atlantic Monthly*, "As We May Think." (This article is available on the Web at `http:/ /www.csi.uottawa.ca/~dduchier/misc/vbush/as-we-may-think.html`.)

The Origins of Hypertext

Bush called his system a *memex* (*mem*ory *ex*tension), and proposed it as a tool to help the human mind cope with information. Having observed that previous inventions had expanded human abilities for dealing with the physical world, Bush wanted his memex to expand human knowledge in a way that took advantage of the associative nature of human thought.

In 1965, Ted Nelson coined the term *hypertext* to describe text that closely followed Bush's model, in that Nelson's text was not constrained to be sequential. Hypertext, as Nelson described, links documents to form a web of relationships that draw on the possibilities for extending and augmenting the meaning of a "flat" piece of text with links to other texts. Hypertext is more than just footnotes that serve as commentary or further information about a text; rather, hypertext extends the structure of ideas by making "chunks of" ideas or information available for inclusion in many parts of multiple texts. Nelson also coined the term *hypermedia*, which is hypertext not constrained to be text. Hypermedia can include expressions of multimedia—pictures, graphics, sound, and movies.

The Origins of the Web

Vannevar Bush's and Ted Nelson's ideas about information systems showed up in another project in the late 1980s. In March 1989, Tim Berners-Lee, a researcher at the Conseil Europeen pour la Recherche Nucleaire (CERN) European Laboratory for Particle Physics in Geneva, Switzerland, proposed a hypertext system to enable efficient information sharing for members of the high energy physics community. Berners-Lee had a background in text processing, real-time software and communications, and had previously developed a hypertext system he called "Enquire" in 1980. Berners-Lee's 1989 proposal, called "HyperText and CERN," circulated for comment. The following were important components of the proposal:

- A user interface that would be consistent across all platforms and that would allow users to access information from many different computers
- A scheme for this interface to access a variety of document types and information protocols
- A provision for "universal access," which would allow any user on the network to access any information

By late 1990, an operating prototype of the World Wide Web ran on a NeXT computer, and a line-mode user interface (called "WWW") was completed. The essential pieces of the Web were in place, although not widely available for network use.

Throughout the early 1990s, interest in the Web grew and spread worldwide. In March 1991, the WWW interface was used on a local network, and by May of that year, it was made available on central CERN machines. On January 15, 1992, the WWW interface became publicly available from CERN, and the CERN team demonstrated the Web to researchers internationally throughout the rest of the year.

Mosaic: The First "Killer" App

In 1993, interest in the Web grew very rapidly. A young undergraduate named Marc Andreessen who was then at the University of Illinois at Urbana-Champaign worked on a project for the National Center for Supercomputing Applications (NCSA), and led a team that developed a browser called "Mosaic" for the Web. The group released an alpha version of Mosaic for the X Window System in February 1993 that was among the first crop of graphical interfaces to the Web. Mosaic, with its fresh look and graphical interface presenting the Web using a point-and-click design, fueled great interest in the Web and online information. By the end of 1993, attendees at the Internet World Conference and Exposition in New York City were eager to learn about graphical interfaces to the Web. The *New York Times* hailed Mosaic as the Internet's "killer application."

In 1994, more commercial players got into the Web game. Companies, including Spry, Inc., announced commercial versions of Web browser software, Marc Andreessen and colleagues left NCSA in March to form, with Jim Clark (former chairman of Silicon Graphics), a company that later became known as Netscape Communications Corporation (`http://home.netscape.com/`). By May 1994, interest in the Web was so intense that the first international conference on the World Wide Web, held in Geneva, overflowed with attendees. By June 1994, there were 1,500 known public Web servers.

By mid-1994, it was clear to the original developers of the Web at CERN that the stable development of the Web should fall under the guidance of an international organization. In July, the Massachusetts Institute of Technology (MIT) and CERN announced the formation of the World Wide Web Consortium, or W³C.

The Web Today

Today, the W³C (`http://www.w3.org/hypertext/WWW/Consortium/`) guides the technical development and standards for the evolution of the Web. The W³C is a consortium of universities and private industries, run by the Laboratory for Computer Science (LCS) at MIT, collaborating with CERN (`http://www.cern.ch/`) and Institut National de Recherche en Informatique et en Automatique (INRIA), a French research institute in computer science (`http://www.inria.fr/`).

In 1995, the development of the Web was marked by rapid commercialization and technical change. Netscape Communication's "Mozilla" browser continued to include more extensions of the Hypertext Markup Language (HTML), and issues of security for commercial cash transactions garnered much attention. By May 1995, there were more than 15,000 known public Web servers, a tenfold increase over the number from a year before. Many companies had joined the W³C by 1995, including, among others, AT&T, Digital Equipment Corporation, Enterprise Integration Technologies, FTP Software, Hummingbird Communication, IBM, MCI, NCSA, Netscape Communications, Novell, Open Market, O'Reilly & Associates, Spyglass, and Sun Microsystems.

By mid-1995, the emergence of the Java and Virtual Reality Modeling Language technologies placed the Web at the start of another cycle of rapid change and alteration. Java, in development for several years at Sun Microsystems, promises to make the Web far more interactive than ever before possible. (See Chapter 1, "Java Makes Executable Content Possible.") Virtual Reality Modeling Language, which can allow developers to model three-dimensional scenes for delivery through special Web browsers, may also dramatically change what the Web has to offer.

A Definition of the World Wide Web

Despite its rapid growth and technical developments, the Web in 1995 retains the essential functional components it had in its 1990 form. Its popularity as a view of the Internet, however, has muddied popular understanding of it, because the Web is sometimes viewed as equivalent to the Internet and browsers are sometimes thought of as equivalent to the Web rather than a view into it. However, the Web is a very distinct system from the Internet and its browsers. First, the Web is not a network, but an application system (a set of software programs). Second, the World Wide Web can be deployed and used on many different kinds of networks (not necessarily just Internet networks) and it can even be used on no network at all or on a local network unconnected to any other.

A Metaphor for the Web

Imagine a library in which all the spines of the books have been removed and the gravity in the building has been turned off, allowing the pages to float freely. If people could connect one page to another using very light threads taped to the pages, this would be similar to the way the Web's hypertext is arranged. Pages free-float, so users might encounter a work from any page within it and reach other works by following the threads leading off a page.

Here is a more technical definition of the Web:

> The World Wide Web is a hypertext information and communication system popularly used on the Internet computer network with data communications operating according to a client/server model. Web clients (browsers) can access multi-protocol and hypermedia information.

Figure 3.1 summarizes the technical organization of the Web based on this definition.

Figure 3.1.
The technical organiza-
tion of the Web.

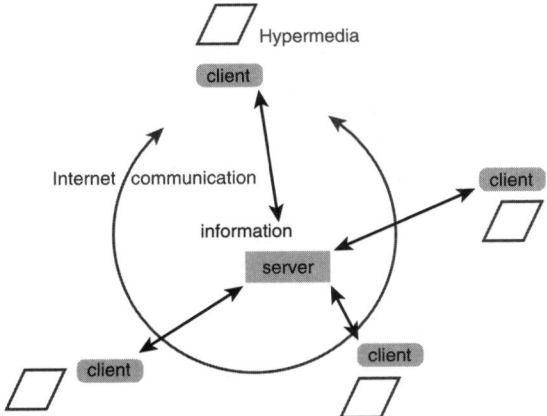

How Does Java Transform the Web?

Java changes the Web by bringing more "intelligence" to Web browsers. Although Java-enabled browsers have user interfaces that are much the same as many other Web browsers, their technical operation marks a significant shift in focus. Java's executable content requires Java-enabled browsers to be smart; that is, they must be able to interpret executable content.

Java Supports Client-Side Interactivity

A *client/server model* for networked computer systems involves three components: the client, the server, and the network. A *client* is a software application that most often runs on the end-user's computer host. A *server* is a software application that most often runs on the information provider's computer host. Client software can be customized to the user's hardware system and it acts as an interface from that system to information provided on the server. The user can initiate a request for information or action through the client software. This request travels over the network to the server. The server interprets the request and takes some desired action. This action might include a database lookup or a change in recorded database information. The results of the requested transaction (if any) are sent back to the client for display to the user. All client/server communication follows a set of rules, or protocols, which are defined for the client/server system. Figure 3.2 summarizes these relationships, showing the flow of a request from a client to a server and the passing back of information from a server to a client. A client might access many servers employing the protocols both the server and client understand.

The distributed form of "request" and "serve" activities of the client/server model allows for many efficiencies. Because the client software interacts with the server according to a pre-defined protocol, the client software can be customized for the user's particular computer host. (The server doesn't have to worry about the hardware particularities of the client software.) For example, a Web client (a browser) can be developed for Macintosh computers that can access any Web server. This same Web server might be accessed by a Web browser written for a UNIX workstation running the X Window System. This makes it easier to develop information because there is a clear demarcation of duties between the client and the server. Separate versions of the information need not be developed for any particular hardware platform because the customizations necessary are written into client software for each platform. An analogy to the client/server model is the television broadcast system. A customer can buy any kind of television set (client) to view broadcasts from any over-the-air broadcast tower (server). Whether the user has a wrist-band TV or a projection screen TV, the set receives information from the broadcast station in a standard format and displays it appropriate to the user's TV set. Separate TV programming need not be created for each kind of set, such as for color or black-and-white sets or different size sets. New television stations that are created will be able to send signals to all the currently-in-use television sets.

Figure 3.2.
A client/server model for data communication.

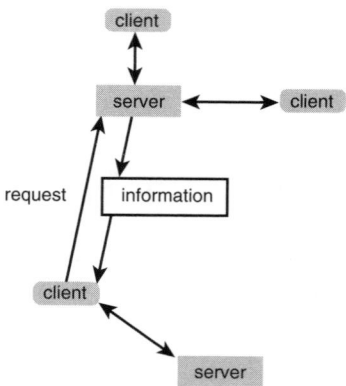

Java brings another dimension to the client/server model. Of course, Java does follow the basic model: a Java-enabled browser is a client that sends requests to Web servers for information. The Java-enabled browser interprets and displays the information sent from the server. This information includes both the hypertext as well as any bytecodes. These bytecodes are Java's new twist on this model. The Java clients execute the content distributed from the servers. These bytecodes, as described in Chapter 2, are also architecture-neutral, just like the other information sent from the Web server.

Java Can Eliminate the Need for Helper Applications

Helper applications include software that a (non-Java-enabled) Web browser invokes to display multimedia information to the user. For example, in order for the user to view movies, the Web browser must have movie-display software installed and available. To display inlined graphical images in an HTML document, the Web browser must be graphical—that is, employ a system such as X Window System, Macintosh Operating System, or Microsoft Windows as a graphical user interface.

Instead of relying on helper applications, programmers developing applets for Java-enabled browsers can create content handlers to handle media formats.

Java Adds to the Web's Communication Contexts and Potential

The Java language and its browsers are part of the larger context for communication on the Web. Whether you write and distribute applets or just observe them, you take part in communication activities and traditions that have been developing on the Web for many years. Because Java is still so new, it has not yet appeared in all Web communication contexts. You'll see more specific examples of Java used on the Web in later chapters of this book. This subsection briefly reviews the Web's context and potential and how Java can be a part of it.

Java and Communication Contexts on the Web

Communication on the Web can take many forms and take place in many contexts. Genres, or traditional ways for communicating, have evolved on the Web. These genres correspond, in many ways, to offline human communication contexts:

■ **Interpersonal**: The Web provides a way for users to create a home page, which typically conveys personal or professional information. The practice of creating a home page emerged from the technical necessity of defining the "default" page that a Web browser displays when requesting information from a Web server when only the host name or a host and directory name is given. Home pages are thus traditionally the top-level page for a server, organization, or individual. When created by individuals, home pages often reveal detailed personal information about their authors and are often listed in directories of home pages. Also, individuals often follow the tradition of linking to colleagues' or friends' pages, creating *electronic tribes.* (Mathematically, these electronic tribes are defined by the cliques of home pages in the directed graph describing the Web.) When used interpersonally, personal home pages offer one-to-one communication, although the technical operation of all pages on the Web is one-to-many.

Personal "applets" have not yet become prominent, but Java may enable individuals to create an excutable "persona" with which other Web users can interact.

■ **Group:** As described in the interpersonal definition, cliques of personal pages can define a particular Web tribe or group. Similarly, people can form associations on the Web that are independent of geography and focused on interest in a common topic. Subject-tree breakdowns of information on the Web often evolve from collaborative linking and the development of resource lists and original material describing a subject. (See the following section's discussion about locating subject-based information on the Web.) Similarly, groups of people associate on the Web based on common interests in communication.

■ **Organizational:** Many of the initial Web servers appearing on the Web belong to an organization, not individuals, so the home page for a server often identifies the institution or organization that owns the server. In this way, the genre of the Campus-Wide Information System (CWIS) evolved on Web servers of educational institutions. Similarly, commercial, governmental, and non-governmental organizations to a large degree have followed the pattern established by CWISs.

Many organizations now use Java in their Web pages to add interest and provide service to users. You see examples of these pages in the next chapter.

■ **Mass:** Just as other media have been used for one-to-many dissemination of information (newspapers, radio, television), so too is the Web used for mass communication. Many commercial and non-commercial magazines and other publications are distributed through the Web. Moreover, as noted previously, all publicly available Web pages are potentially readable to anyone using the Web, and are thus potentially one-to-many communications.

Java is being used actively for mass communication, as shown in the example from the *NandO Times* in Chapter 1.

The key concept to understand is that the Web as a communication system can be flexibly used to communicate in a variety of ways. The classification of the communication (in the categories listed) depends on who is taking part in the communication. The exact classification of any expression on the Web can be blurred by the potentially global reach of any Web page. Thus, a personal home page may be used interpersonally, but it may be accessed far more times on the Web than a publication created and intended for mass consumption. Java's capability for delivering interactive content adds new possiblities to each of these categories.

Java and the Web's Potential

The Web is a flexible system for communication that can be used in many contexts, ranging from individual communication on home pages through group communication and mass communication. In addition to these contexts, the Web also serves the following functions:

- **Information Delivery:** A Web browser provides the user with a "viewer" to look into FTP space, Gopher space, or hypertext information on the Web. The structure of hypertext enables user selectivity because of the many ways a user can choose to follow links in hypertext. Java adds the potential for new protocol handlers and content handlers.

- **Communication:** People can use Web hypertext to create forums for sharing information, discussion, and helping group members make contact with each other. Java's executable content introduces new forms of more interactive communication.

- **Interaction:** Using gateway programming, a Web developer can build some degree of interactivity into an application, providing the user with a way to receive customized information based on queries. Gateway programs can also allow a user to change or add to an information structure. A higher degree of interactivity is possible using Java because of its executable content.

- **Computation:** Also using gateway programming, the Web can be used to provide an interface to other applications and programs for information processing. Based on user selections, a Web application can return a computed or customized result through a gateway program. Java programmers can create software for computation that can be distributed and executed.

The symbols shown in figure 3.3 can be used to illustrate some of the previously listed Web functions.

Using the symbols in figure 3.3, figure 3.4 shows the important distinction between selectivity and gateway programming interactivity. When the user accesses the Web server on the left, content is presented using hypertext. The links in the hypertext pages give the user a great deal of choice, or selectivity, for encountering information in the database. However, no information is customized to user inputs or computed based on user requests. Although this server offers the user great flexibility in information retrieval because of the hypertext design of its pages, this server is not interactive.

The key to the level of interactivity, as shown in the server on the right, is that the executable program accepts input from the user through a Web page. Based on these user inputs, this executable can compute a result and (possibly, also using information from the database) return this customized information result to the user. Moreover, the executable program also allows the user to (possibly) change the contents of the database, or make some other change in the database or files on the server. These changes might include altering the structure or contents of hypertext or the contents of other files. The construction of this executable program requires skills in gateway programming.

Java adds still another level of interactivity. Instead of the server computing a result, the Java-enabled browser is the mechanism for computation.

Figure 3.3.
Symbols for representing Web functions.

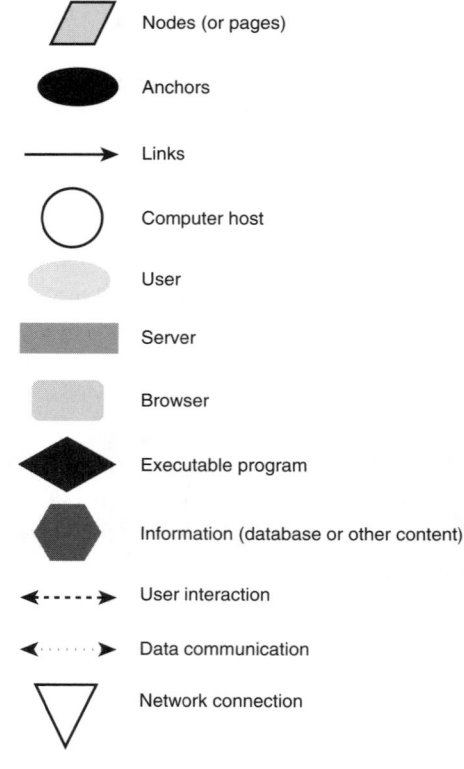

Nodes (or pages)

Anchors

Links

Computer host

User

Server

Browser

Executable program

Information (database or other content)

User interaction

Data communication

Network connection

Figure 3.4.
Web selectivity and gateway interactivity.

Selectivity   Interactivity

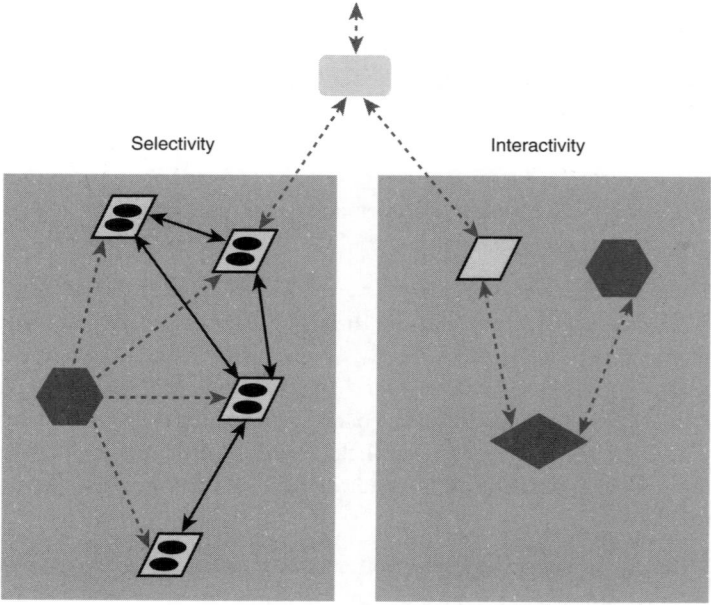

Chapter Summary

■ The Web emerged from ideas about the associative, non-linear organization of information. Java is another step in this evolution.

■ The Web is a hypertext information and communication system popularly used on the Internet in a client/server model, offering hypermedia display capabilities through appropriate browsers, some of which require helper applications.

■ Java-capable browsers bring client-side interactivity and computation to the Web and can eliminate the need for helper applications.

■ Communication on the Web can assume many forms and take place in many contexts, ranging from individual communication to group and mass communication. Java can potentially augment the Web's communication contexts and functions.

PART II

Exploring Java's Potential

This book makes much of Java's transformative power for Web communication. The three chapters in this part get very specific about exactly what *transformative power* means, presenting many examples that bring Web pages to life in different ways.

Chapter 4 examines how animation on Web pages can range from simple moving letters to elaborate cartoons or instructional applications. With Java programming, text or graphics on Web pages can scroll, move, or repeat a programmed routine. Java can also implement the equivalent of a graphical imagemap.

Chapter 5 examines the interactive side of Java, showing how user response can shape the flow of information processing in an applet, making specialized learning tutorials possible. Java is also useful for creating *virtual scientific instruments* as applets, giving users the chance to explore and learn scientific concepts by interacting with an applet that models a real-world phenomenon.

Finally, Chapter 6 explores the distributed network communication possibilities of Java. Java's applets make possible the delivery of executable content, as well as new protocols and formats. Java also enables the dynamic retrieval of network information, making Web browser autopilots or guided tours possible.

You'll gain the following from these chapters:

- Knowledge of the basic ways that Java can animate Web pages, including specific examples of applets and how you can use the HTML APP tag to include these on Web pages
- A sense of how Java's interactivity makes instantaneous, customized user response possible
- An appreciation for how Java distributes content; how programmers create new protocol or content handlers; and the basics of network information retrieval with Java

CHAPTER 4

Java Animates Web Pages

The Java language and Java-enabled browsers allow a more visually dynamic Web than previously possible. Instead of hypertext pages containing only still images with helper applications to display video, Java Web pages can include animated graphics, text, and any moving visual elements a Java programmer can dream up.

This chapter surveys several Java applets that implement animation. In some cases, the chapter also includes key portions of the source code to demonstrate how these applets are made. If you want to understand these code portions in more detail, you can read more about Java programming basics in Part IV of this book. If not, you can skip over the programming sections for now and return to them after reading Part IV. If you'd like to try out the applets described here, you should be familiar with Java's connection with HTML as described in Chapter 2.

The purpose of this chapter is to familiarize you with the many types of animation possible using applets. If you are ready to place applets on your Web pages, this chapter will also be invaluable to you; it contains instructions for including some publicly available demonstration applets that you can customize and include on a hypertext page.

Applets in Motion

If you are a new user of a Java-enabled browser, you will immediately notice that some Java pages contain moving text, figures, and animations. These moving images are made possible by Java applets that implement Java's Runnable interface. These applets don't just display static text or graphics; they can execute their content continuously.

NervousText

One example of animated text is the NervousText applet, originally developed by Daniel Wyszynski at the Center for Applied Large-Scale Computing. Wyszynski's NervousText applet displays HotJava! in jostling on-screen letters. David Leach modified this applet so that it can display any programmer-defined string. Figure 4.1 shows Wyszynski's and David Leach's NervousText applets on a Web page.

Figure 4.1.
The NervousText applet. (Courtesy of Daniel Wyszynski and David Leach)

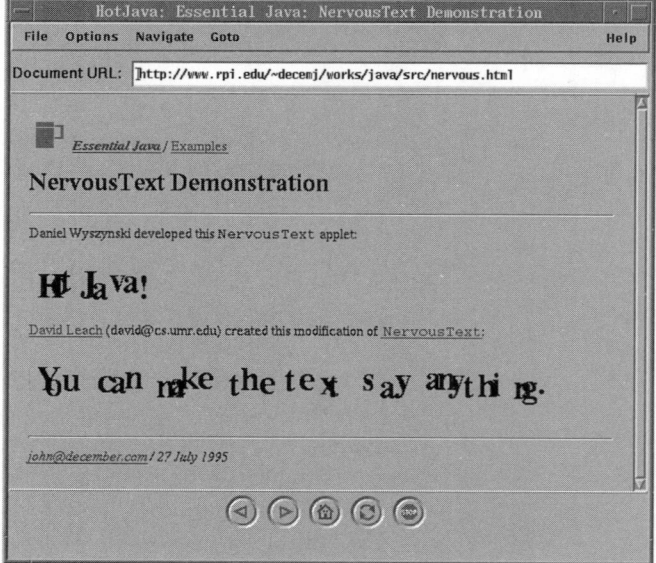

The NervousText applet is a good demonstration of how an applet can be included on any Web page, not just Web pages created by the applet's developer. You are not limited to using only applets that you write. You can modify and use other developers' applets from their sites, just as you link to hypertext pages at other sites. In fact, sharing applets across the Net is what Java's capability to distribute executable content is all about.

You use the APP element in HTML to place a publicly available applet in a Web page. The APP element can identify a Java class anywhere on a publicly available server on the Net. The APP element specifies the applet's location and class name. The HTML file in the HotJava browser shown in figure 4.1 uses the following HTML elements:

```
<APP Src="http://java.sun.com/applets/applets/NervousText/"
     Class="NervousText">

<APP Src   = "http://www.cs.umr.edu/~david/java/"
     Class = "NervousText"
     msg   = "You can make the text say anything.">
```

The attributes of the APP tag, Class and Src, identify the applet's class (NervousText) and location. Wyszynski's original applet is stored at Sun Microsystems site at http://java.sun.com/applets/applets/NervousText/classes/NervousText.class. David's modification is at http://www.cs.umr.edu/~david/java/classes/NervousText.class.

The line in the second applet

```
msg   = "You can make the text say anything."
```

is a way of specifying an attribute of an applet. You can set these attributes in an HTML file just like attributes of other HTML elements. When the Java-enabled browser reads the APP tag, it passes the values of these attributes to the applet itself.

Using Java Applets without Java

You can put together a Web page that includes applets using the APP element without using the HotJava browser or the Java compiler. You need only the compiled class file to serve applets. If you use applets that are at remote locations, you need to identify where on the Net the bytecode file for the applet exists. To do so, use the Src attribute of the APP element. Of course, users who do not have a HotJava browser cannot observe the applets.

If you use a remote applet repeatedly, consider downloading and serving a copy of the class file from your own site. Before taking this step, however, check with the information provider. And, of course, check out the applet's behavior—it is executable content and runs on the computer of anyone requesting to view it.

David Leach's modification of NervousText demonstrates the programming technique of obtaining the values of attributes. In the Java applet code, David uses the getAttribute method to find out the value of the msg attributes passed from the HTML APP element to the Java applet. David's class definition includes the data string userString; and the init() method includes this line:

```
userString = getAttribute("msg");
```

David uses this string in the paint() method to derive the characters that draw the applet. The trick of making the letters "nervous" is to vary their coordinates in the paint() method by using a random number generator for their X and Y coordinates:

```
x_coord = (int) (Math.random()*10+15*i);
y_coord = (int) (Math.random()*10+36);
```

TickerTape

Similar to the NervousText applet is another good demonstration of Java's animation capabilities: TickerTape. The applet was originally developed by Sven Heinicke at *HotWired* and later modified by David Leach and John Stone at the University of Missouri-Rolla. You can modify TickerTape by setting attributes in an HTML page. These attributes include the following:

Attribute	Explanation
MSGS = String	Message string to display
WIDTH = int	Width of the string display
RED = int	Value for red color of text (in range 0-256)
BLUE = int	Value for blue color of text (in range 0-256)
FNT = name	Name for font to display the text
GREEN = int	Value for green color of text (in range 0-256)
SPEED = int	The number of pixels to move the message per cycle
REST = int	How long to wait before moving message (milliseconds)

You can set these attributes in HTML; here's an example setup of three TickerTapes:

```
<P><APP Src = "http://www.hotwired.com/java/"
    Class = "TickerTape"
    msgs  = "This is an example of a ticker tape"
    width = "100">

<P><APP Src = "http://www.hotwired.com/java/"
    Class = "TickerTape"
    msgs  = "Several tickers can be on a page"
    red   = "0"      blue  = "256"   green = "100"
    width = "500"
    fnt   = "Helvetica"
    size  = "30">

<P><APP Src  = "http://www.hotwired.com/java/"
    Class = "TickerTape"
    msgs  = "... and have different colors, fonts, and sizes..."
    red   = "5"  blue = "6" green = "250"
    width = "500"
    speed = "25"
    rest  = "2"
    fnt   = "Courier"
    size  = "72">
```

Are Java Users Wasting Bandwidth?

After a Java applet's bytecodes have been downloaded across the network, the user's host is the processor that executes them. The information provider's host works only to distribute the bytecodes. Users of applets, therefore, might typically use far less bandwidth and far less time on the information provider's computer than might Web surfers.

Also, class files containing bytecodes aren't all that large. For example, the TickerTape applet (figure 4.2) is 3,186 bytes—easily smaller than many graphics files routinely downloaded from the *HotWired* server. Therefore, although users may see more action with applets, they are not *necessarily* using more bandwidth on the Web. Of course, leaving a browser on autopilot (such as in the Surf-o-Matic applet in Chapter 6) and walking away would cause a browser to use much bandwith for downloading Web pages.

Information providers must be very careful about the size and processing power required by their applets; a CPU-intensive applet could bring the user's computer to its knees.

Figure 4.2 shows the display of the resulting TickerTape (frozen for the image). The text in the lines scrolls continuously to the left; with the bottom ticker line moving very rapidly.

Figure 4.2.
TickerTape Applet example. (Courtesy of Sven Heinicke, David Leach, and John Stone)

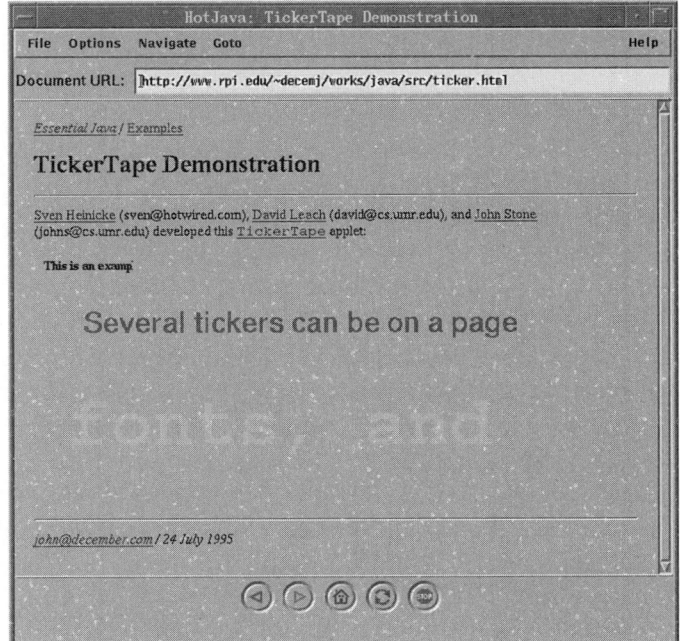

The TickerTape applet uses a key programming trick to cause the letters to move. The code changes the X position of the string by an amount equal to the speed attribute prior to repainting the string in each cycle. Here's the code to do this:

```
xpos -= speed;
```

This line of code subtracts the value of speed from the current horizontal position of the string. The line is a quick way of writing the equivalent xpos = xpos - speed.

Fireworks

Another variation on animation is to have graphics—rather than words only—flash across a page. Erik Wistrand has created an applet that transforms a Web page into a fireworks show (figure 4.3).

Figure 4.3.
*Fireworks Applet
example. (Courtesy
of Erik Wistrand)*

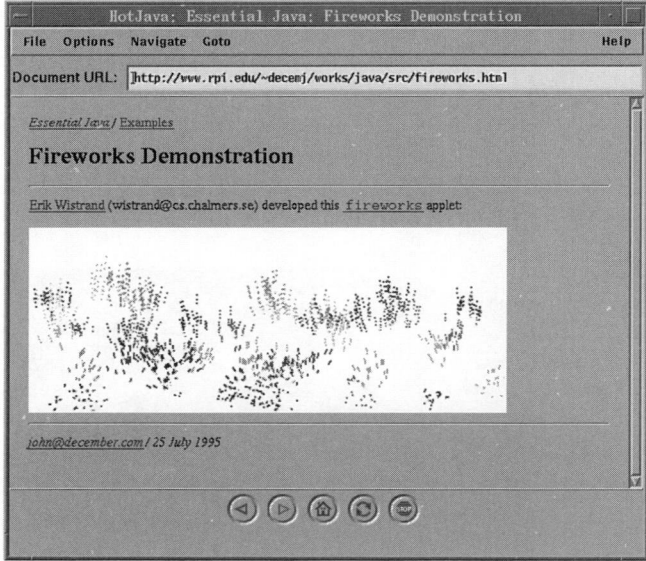

Similar to the TickerTape applet, you can include the Fireworks applet on a Web page, and you can control aspects of its appearance. The Fireworks parameters are as follows:

Attribute	Explanation
ROCKETS = int	Number of rockets to animate (default 3)
POINTS = int	Number of points in each rocket (default 3)
POINTSIZE = int	Pixelsize of points (default 2)
LIFELENGTH = int	Duration of rockets, counted in number of frames (default 100)
GRAV = int	Gravity; large value => rockets fall down fast (default 10)

DELAY = int	Delay in milliseconds between frames (default 50)
TRAIL = int	Number of trailing points (default 10)
COLOR = rrggbb	Red, green, and blue hexidecimal triple for applet background (default is browser background)
WIDTH = int	Applet width in pixels (default tiny = browser default?)
HEIGHT = int	Applet height in pixels (default tiny = browser default?)

Here is the HTML code for including the Fireworks applet on a page:

```
<P>
<APP Src        = "http://www.cs.chalmers.se/~wistrand/"
     Class      = "fireworks"
     ROCKETS    = "50"
     POINTS     = "20"
     LIFELENGTH = "30"
     GRAV       = "20"
     DELAY      = "3"
     POINTSIZE  = "2"
     TRAIL      = "4"
     COLOR      = "ffebcd"
     WIDTH      = "500"
     HEIGHT     = "200"
     >
```

This example sets a series of 50 rockets on a page (shown in figure 4.3). The COLOR attribute uses hexidecimal (base 16) notation to describe the red, green, and blue values of the background image color.

Animation

Not all animations involve moving text for aesthetic purposes. Other animations occur in instructional pages or as part of a user's interaction with a Web page.

Juggling

Chris Seguin has created a juggling instructional page (http://www.acm.uiuc.edu/webmonkeys/Juggling/) that effectively uses animation to *show*—rather than *tell*—how to juggle. You see the juggling page in figure 4.4. Viewed through a HotJava browser, the page shows the two model hands juggling one, two, and three balls.

One of the programming keys in Chris's applet source code is his use of arrays to store the path of the balls. He uses the same ball graphic and repositions it along this path. This is unlike a cartoon in which individual frames would show a ball in its different positions on its path.

Java programmers use both the technique of using a path for a graphic and frames of graphics to animate graphics. In general, the graphic and path approach leads to less memory drain and more flexibility. Although for complicated or animated images (refer back to Duke in Chapter 1), the frame approach is desirable.

Figure 4.4.
*The Java juggling page.
(Courtesy of Chris
Seguin)*

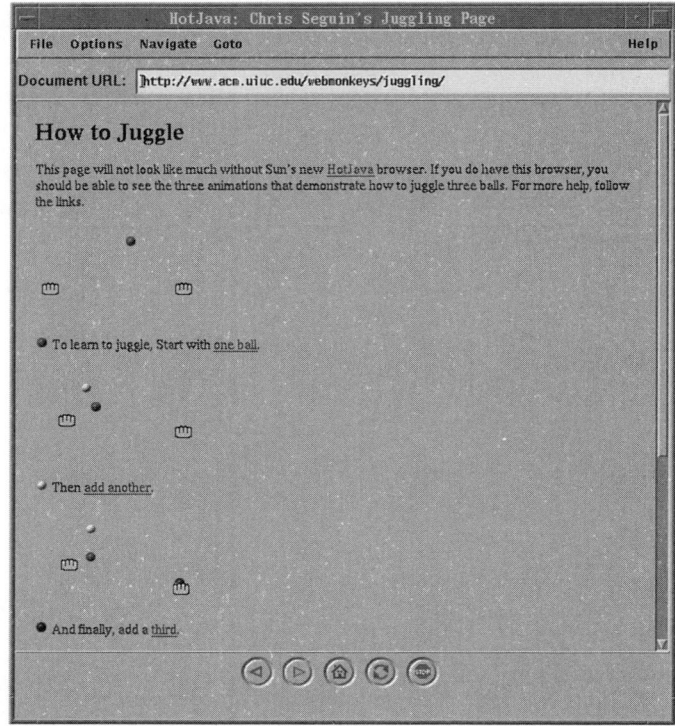

Drawing on Famous Pictures

Another variation in graphics on Web pages is to let you draw right on pictures on a page.
Johan van der Hoeven has created the Magic applet, which has a fanciful appeal. You can use
it to draw on famous pictures as if you were using a magic marker. Figure 4.5 shows markings
on a world map and the *Mona Lisa*.

Here is the HTML code demonstrating Johan's Magic applet. Note that the image can be located anywhere on the Web:

```
<H2>Draw on the World</H2>

<APP Class    = "Magic"
     Src      = "http://www.rosebud.com/rb/art/jo/"
     imgurl   = "http://www.rpi.edu/~decemj/images/world.gif"
     linecolor = "red">

<H2>Draw on the <CITE>Mona Lisa</CITE></H2>

<APP Class    = "Magic"
     Src      = "http://www.rosebud.com/rb/art/jo/"
     imgurl   = "http://www.paris.org/Musees/Louvre/Treasures/gifs/MonaLisaa.gif"
     linecolor = "blue">
```

Figure 4.5.
*Marking on the world
and the* Mona Lisa.
*(Courtesy of Johan van
der Hoeven)*

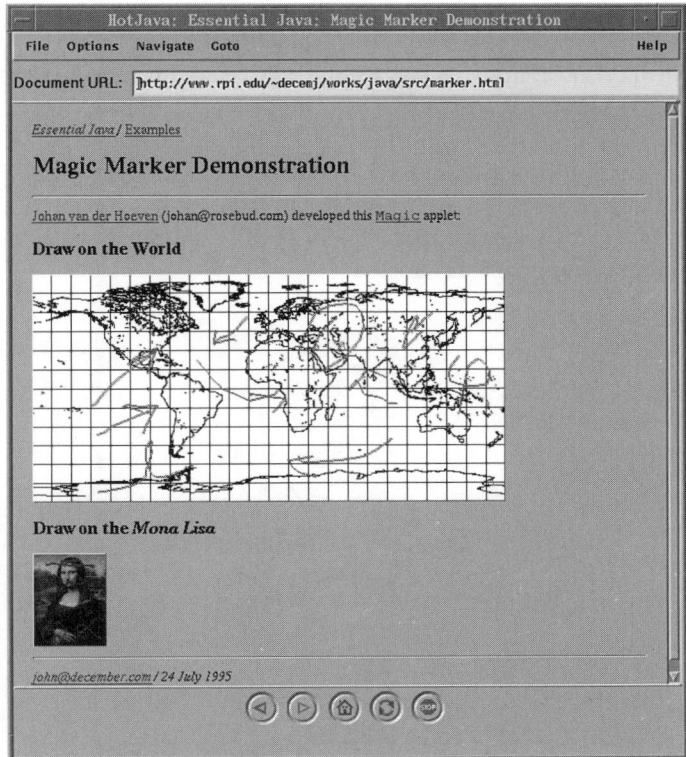

Who Owns What?

The drawing applet in this section demonstrates the blending of authorship and ownership that Java is opening on the Web. The author of the HTML page used an applet written by one person and an image created by another (and painted by still another—Leonardo Da Vinci—long ago!) to create an environment for the user to alter the image. Who is the author of the resulting Web page and who finally owns the melded pieces? The talent of the Java programmer who made the applet? The Web page creator who put the pieces together? The browser manufacturer? The user who marks the image? The creator of the original image? Da Vinci perhaps never would have imagined his painting would be transmitted around the world to be defaced with such glee. These questions raise just some of the legal and intellectual property issues involved in the use of Java and the Web.

A Live Feedback ImageMap

Still another variation on Java graphics is to make images function just like HTML imagemaps; when the user clicks on certain parts of the image, other resources are retrieved. Jim Graham at Sun Microsystems has implemented an applet to demonstrate this capability. Shown in figure 4.6, this applet demonstrates the equivalent functionality of an HTML imagemap, but with the additional features of live feedback. When a user passes the cursor over a "hot" region of the image, that region appears highlighted to indicate that clicking on it will retrieve another resource or some media content.

Figure 4.6.
*Live Feedback
ImageMap. (Courtesy of
Jim Graham, Sun
Microsystems)*

Commercial Sites Using Java

The demonstrations in this chapter show many of Java's animation capabilities. But Java is more than a good show; it is also already at work on commercial Web sites. *The NandO Times* uses Java (refer to figure 1.13), as does George Coates Performance Works (refer to figure 1.10), ESPNET SportsZone (refer to figure 1.14), Dimension X (http://www.dimensionx.com/), *HotWired* (http://www.hotwired.com/), and Sun Microsystems (http://www.sun.com/). Because Java brings so much visual interest to a Web page, it has great potential to draw attention, convey specialized information, and provide entertainment.

The Rolling Stones

The Rolling Stones made a big splash on the Internet Multicast Backbone (MBONE—http://www.eit.com/techinfo/mbone/mbone.html) when they used it to simulcast part of their November 18, 1994, Dallas Cotton Bowl concert. Today, the Stones Web site (http://www.stones.com/) is making a splash with Java.

The Stones site contains several interesting Java applets:

- A Stones puzzle (http://www.stones.com/javapuzzle.html), in which you slide the squares to make the famous tongue logo.
- The Stones Java devil (http://www.stones.com/new.html), which animates the What's New page for the site.
- On the opening page of the Stones Voodoo Lounge (http://www.stones.com/javaindex.html), animated flags that move back and forth across the screen. This page is shown in figure 4.7.

Figure 4.7.
*The Rolling Stones
Voodoo Lounge with
Java. (Courtesy of
Stephan Fitch and John
Graham)*

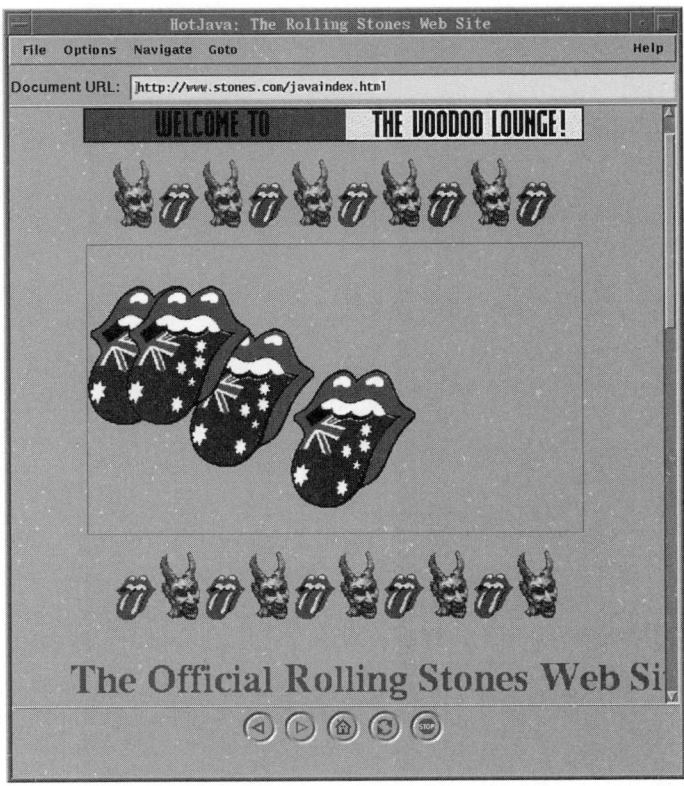

Accurate Information System Consultant

Other commercial providers are using Java to add interest to their pages through animation. Accurate Information Systems (http://accurate.com.my/) uses Java to greet users with a moving ticker tape and a bouncing ball (figure 4.8).

Of course, just as the BLINK tag and other graphics elements become overused to the point of excess on the Web, so might applets be used gratuitously. The potential for applets to add motion, interest, information, and real service to users of a Web is great, however, and we have yet to realize Java's full potential.

Figure 4.8.
Accurate Information System Consultant tickertape greeting. (Courtesy of Accurate Information System Consultant)

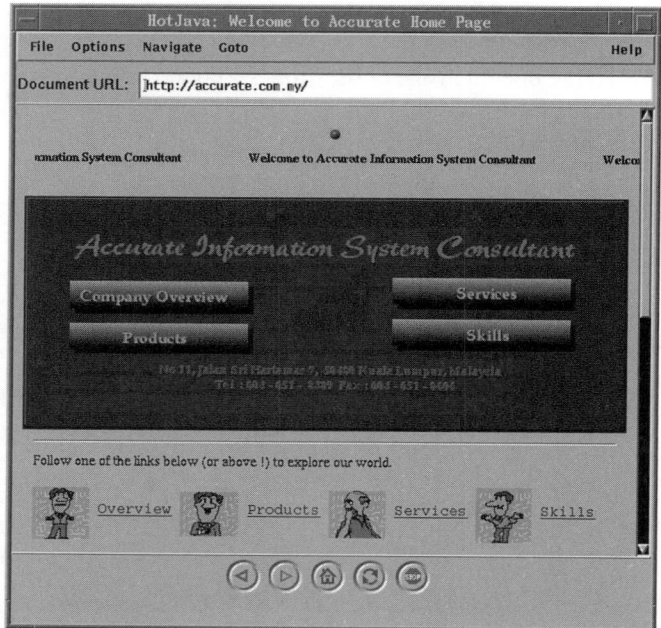

Chapter Summary

You can use Java applets to place animations on Web pages. A user can set the parameters of an existing applet using the APP element and bring an applet to his or her own web page. Developers can create new applets to provide this functionality and make them available for users.

- Text can shimmer using NervousText. Users can include this applet on their pages by using the APP element. By setting attributes of the applet, the user can control characteristics and behavior of the applet.
- Text can scroll, as shown in the TickerTape applet.

- Graphics can repeat a visual pattern, such as in the Fireworks applet.

- Moving applets can teach a lesson, as in the Juggling applet.

- The Magic applet enables users to alter graphics, allowing them to draw on an image.

- A Java applet can perform the equivalent function of an HTML imagemap. Java's advantage over traditional imagemaps is that Java imagemaps can give instant feedback regarding the user's cursor position. Feedback does not need to be delayed until after a mouse click.

- Many companies already use Java, including rock bands and computer companies, to provide interest on Web pages.

CHAPTER 5

Java Makes Web Pages Interactive

Java's capability to animate Web pages is just the surface of what you might first notice when experiencing the Web through a Java-enabled browser. Not only do items *move* on Java Web pages, but applets can also accept user input through mouse clicks or keyboard entries. Java enables people to create Web pages with embedded crossword puzzles, oscilloscopes, chemical models, games, and even communication systems. (For some illlustrations of these, refer to the figures in Chapter 1.)

This chapter surveys some Java applets that provide interactivity. These Java applets range from simple games to instructional modules. Because, as of this writing, Java is still in its infancy, this chapter shows just a glimpse of the rich interactivity Java may bring to the Web.

This chapter also points out key programming tricks used in each of these applets. You can learn more about the basics of programming in Java and how to make use of the tricks in your own applets in Part IV, "Developing Java Applications."

What is Interactivity?

The word *interactivity* has become a buzzword in media development. Products claim they have it, and developers promise to bring interactivity to various media (television, CD-ROMs, magazines, newspapers, games, and so on). Interactivity has been promised so much that it is nearly as hollow a term as *information superhighway*—meaning very little and lacking specific illustrations.

A dictionary definition touches on the main idea of mutual response and reciprocality:

in-ter-ac-tive adj 1. mutually or reciprocally active; 2. of, relating to, or being a two-way electronic communication system (as a telephone, cable television, or a computer) that involves a user's orders (as for information or merchandise) or responses (as to a poll). *(Definition from the online Webster's Dictionary.)*

In the broadest sense of the word, nearly everything could be considered interactive. Toasters and televisions, for example, respond based on a user's orders.

Richer levels of interactivity, however, involve more than response to user's orders; the *level* and *quality* of these responses makes a big difference. The pre-Java Web provided a great deal of user *selectivity* through hypertext links; but its level of interactivity was fairly low. Gateway (Common Gateway Interface, or CGI) programming provides a higher degree of interactivity by making it possible to customize responses to users. Gateway programs are not continuously active, however, because they require the user to click an input button before the user's selections can be processed and a response can be sent.

Java raises the interactive quality of the Web by making possible immediate and continuous stimuli to the user. At the same time, a Java applet can continuously accept and process input from the user. Java can also respond to this direct input and respond with customized feedback. Thus, the Web has become richly interactive with the advent of the Java age.

Interactive Games

Games are a popular application for programmers to create. Games naturally fit into the give-and-take flow that Java applets make possible. Games fit well into the tireless, continuos looping possible in a Java program. The game applets described in this chapter are among the earliest Java applets, yet they display the interactivity Java can bring to Web pages.

Hang Duke

Patrick Chan at Sun Microsystems developed an applet called Hang Duke; the applet has been distributed with the Java browser as a demonstration. Figure 5.1 shows Duke, the mascot of Java. Notice that the user couldn't guess the word; consequently, Duke is in an advanced hanging stage.

Figure 5.1.
The Hang Duke game.
(Courtesy of Patrick
Chan, Sun
Microsystems)

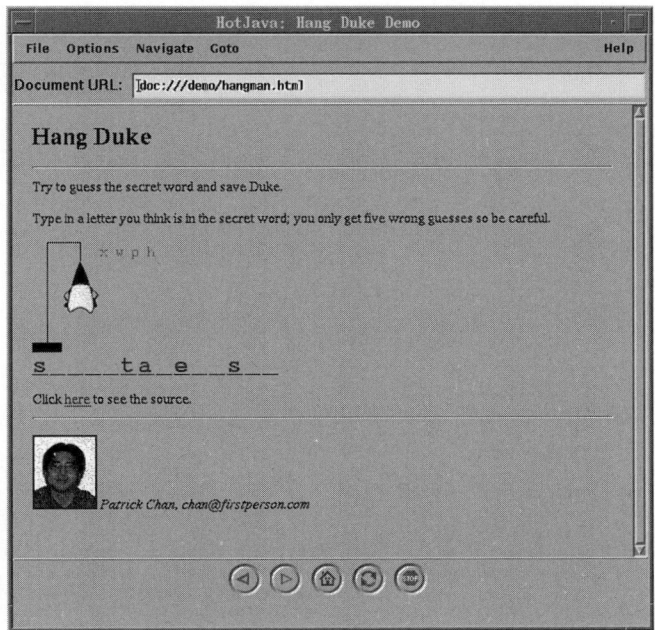

The applet accepts input from the keyboard and displays correct letters in the appropriate slots in the word; each incorrect letter appears near the top of the gallows, and for each wrong letter, another part of Duke's form is drawn.

The Hang Duke applet demonstrates how the simple metaphor of pencil-and-paper game translates easily to the Web with Java.

Hang Duke is a runnable applet. A key part of its source code accepts letters from the user through a method that detects key presses:

```
public void keyDown(int keyPressed)
```

The parameter `keyPressed` is an integer representing a character. This code can be changed to a character and placed in a string expression by casting, like this: `(char)keyPressed`.

Video Poker

Video poker is another familiar game that Java can enable you to transfer easily to the Web. Carl Haynes developed an applet that mimics the mechanical/electronic machine version of a paper card game of chance. The metaphor for the interface is *tactile*: the user punches buttons on the interface using the cursor as the pointer and mouse clicks as the activator. Figure 5.2 shows the game's interface. The user can place a bet, and then draw a hand. Given the five cards, the user can hold some and have the rest replaced. The final hand pays back according to its rank within possible hands, with the payout defined by the table at the top of the applet.

Figure 5.2.
Video poker imple-
mented in Java.
(Courtesy of Carl
Haynes)

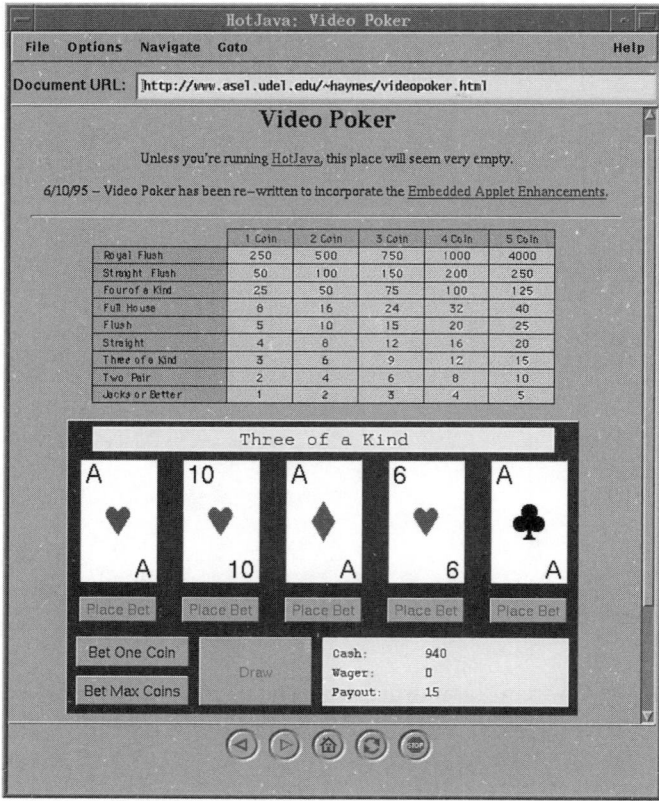

The video poker applet uses a set of classes called HotJava Embedded Applet Enhancements, developed by Jonathan Payne; see http://www.starwave.com/people/jpayne/java/ for more information. This library of classes helps Java developers create more powerful applications more easily. The key is that building good libraries of classes can encapsulate the details of interactive applications. Each application then does not need to be written from scratch; instead, only its unique features need to be expressed. These class structures are the key to building powerful applications.

Educational Applications

The Java game applets described so far in this chapter are innovative in that they use Java technology to enable users to interact with Web pages. This interactivity can also be put to a more exciting use: education. Educators have been adopting the Web for several years now for course-support webs, information about their schools, and even instructional modules. However, the Web's static text, its relatively low level of interactivity, and its limited capabilities for multimedia have made it useful for information delivery but not as amenable to creating truly innovative, engaging applications. This section highlights some early Java applications that highlight its potential for education.

Fractal Figures

Fractals are geometric shapes whose individual parts resemble the whole shape. Fractals can be generated by starting from a basic shape, and then changing the shape based on patterns that are based on the structure of the overall shape. Snowflakes are like fractals: their form at the lowest level of detail reflects a crystalline pattern similar to the whole shape. Because fractals are so hard to explain in words, what a better candidate for a Java application?

Jim Graham at Sun Microsystems has created a Java applet that *shows* how an algorithm generates a fractal. (Check out http://java.sun.com/applets/applets/fractal/index.html.) Figures 5.3, 5.4, and 5.5 show this applet. The top panel displays a rendering of a snowflake curve. Starting from a simple peaked line (figure 5.3), more peaks are added on the line segments until the entire curve resembles the ragged, yet precisely intricate snowflake shape (progressing through figure 5.4 and figure 5.5).

Similarly, the bottom fractal shown in figures 5.3 to 5.5 is called a *Hilbert curve*. Starting with a set of lines forming a *Y*, the algorithm adds detail until the entire fractal appears similar to a fine oriental rug—a pattern like a maze formed from a precise algorithm.

Figure 5.3.
Fractal lesson, initial state. (Courtesy of Jim Graham, Sun Microsystems)

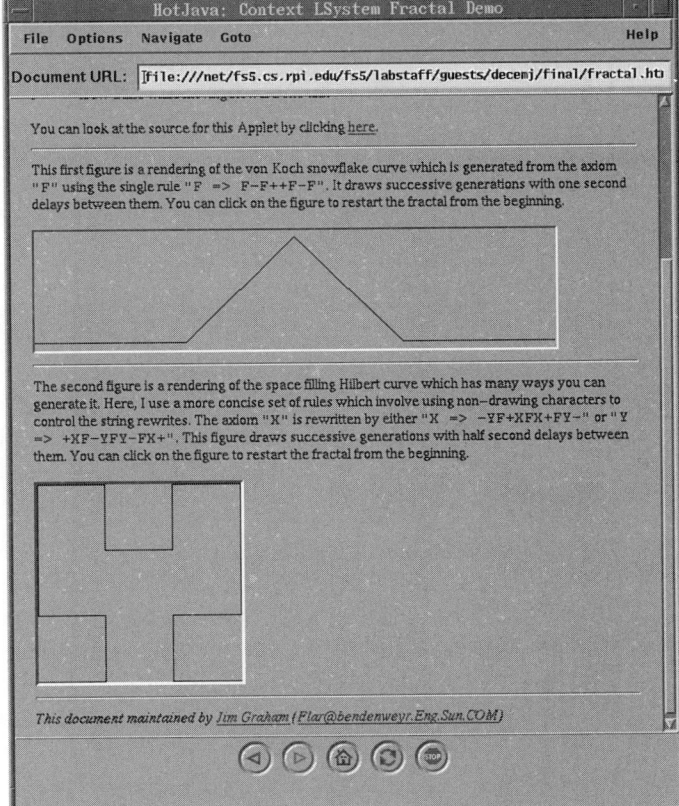

Figure 5.4.
Fractal lesson, middle state. (Courtesy of Jim Graham, Sun Microsystems)

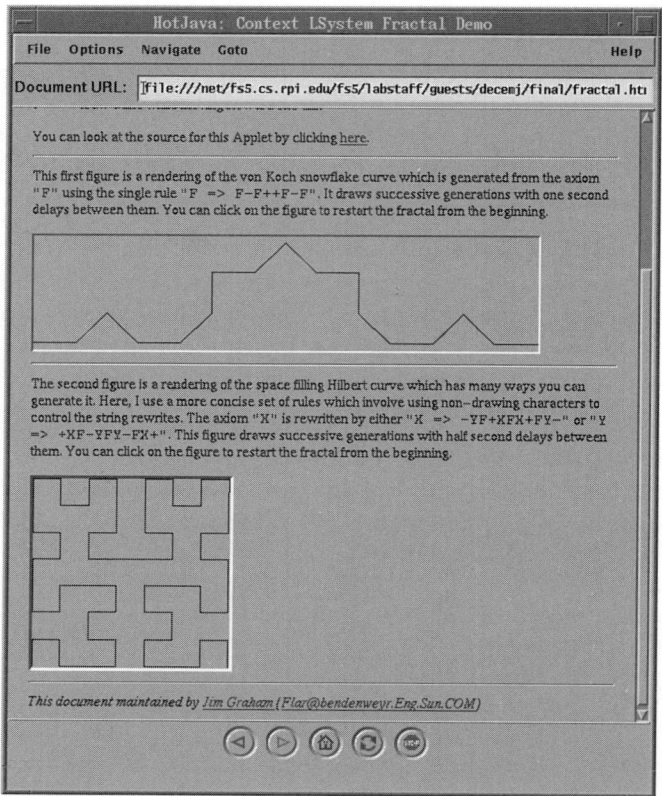

The progression of these fractals from their starting points to their ending points is key: an instructional module could show the stages frozen in images embedded in a Web page (much like the frozen illustrations in this book). However, the Java demonstration allows the user to restart the image, watch it over and over, and get a feel for the progression of the algorithm. The user sees the algorithm in action rather than just imagining how it works.

Word Match Game

The tireless capability of a Java applet to execute an algorithm over and over for the instruction of the user also shows up in the word match game developed by Patrick Chan at Sun Microsystems (figure 5.6). This game is a demonstration of what could be made even more elaborate. Users match pictures with words in foreign languages. To play this game, you first find a picture of an object you recognize. Then, click on the picture of that object, and then click on the corresponding word. The words can appear in many different languages, and so playing the game builds your vocabulary. The applet draws lines from the picture to the word. Once you've completed matching all the words, you then click on the Score button and the applet reports the number of correct matches. The game also has a speaker icon available, so you can hear the pronunciation of the words in some of the languages.

Figure 5.5.
Fractal lesson, final state. (Courtesy of Jim Graham, Sun Microsystems)

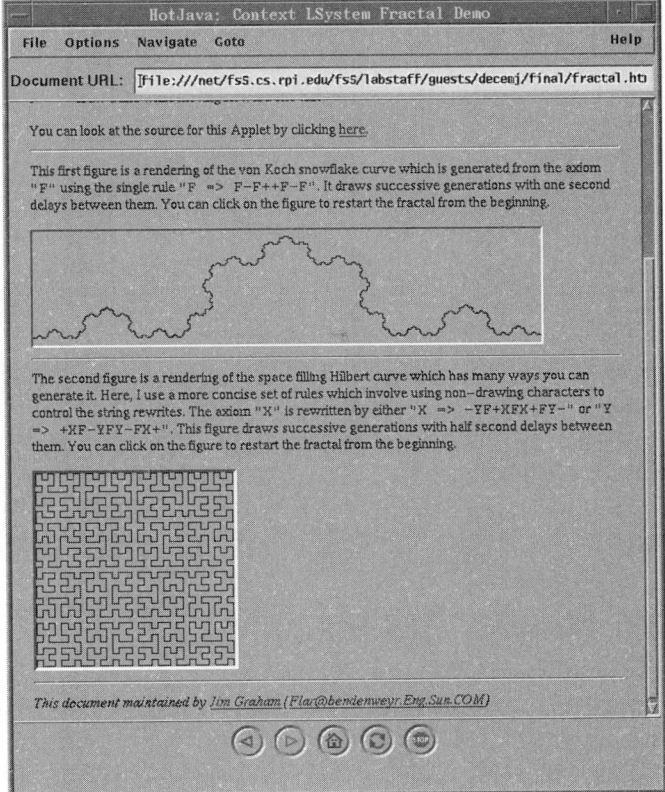

Many languages are available in this applet, as shown in the box to the left. Once you solve the puzzle, you can see it as solved in all the languages by clicking on the language name.

Just like the fractals demonstration, the word match game shows how interactive and multimedia content can give users a place to play on a Web page rather than just observe and select. Neither lesson is meant to be a comprehensive tutorial; instead, each is a demonstration of Java's possibilities. Even as they are, however, the applets are fairly instructive.

Figure 5.6.
Word game lesson.
(Courtesy of Patrick
Chan, Sun
Microsystems)

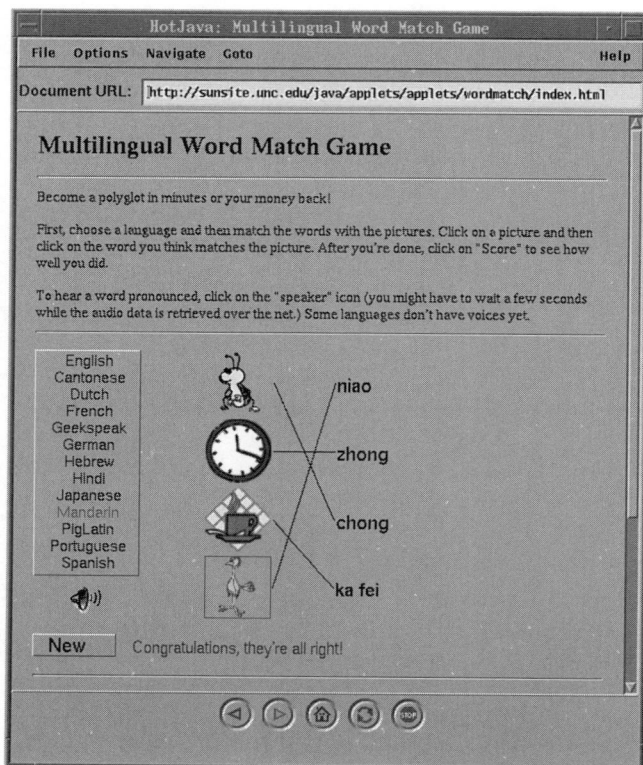

Fast Fourier Transform

The playground for users of Java pages can also include applets that perform complex computations and simulations. Through these applets, users can gain immediate feedback into processes. A good example of such a simulation is the Fast Fourier Transform (FFT) lesson developed by Gopal Chand, David Nicol, and Calum Smeaton (http://www.cee.hw.ac.uk/~calum/java/fft.html). Fourier transforms are used in science and engineering to analyze data or signals. The FFT lessons (figure 5.7) gives users a way to directly see the result of a Fourier Transform calculation. Given a set of input data points on a wave form, the FFT applet calculates and displays the resulting power spectrum.

This FFT application, like the others shown in this chapter, reinforces concepts by providing direct experience to users. With sufficient programming work (the FFT application involved over 700 lines of Java code), a Java Web page can become a sophisticated scientific laboratory for learning. Given more time and experience, as well as more class libraries, educators using Java will be able to add new dimensions to their instructional materials delivered over the Web.

Figure 5.7.
Fast Fourier Transform Lesson. (Courtesy of Gopal Chand, David Nicol, and Calum Smeaton)

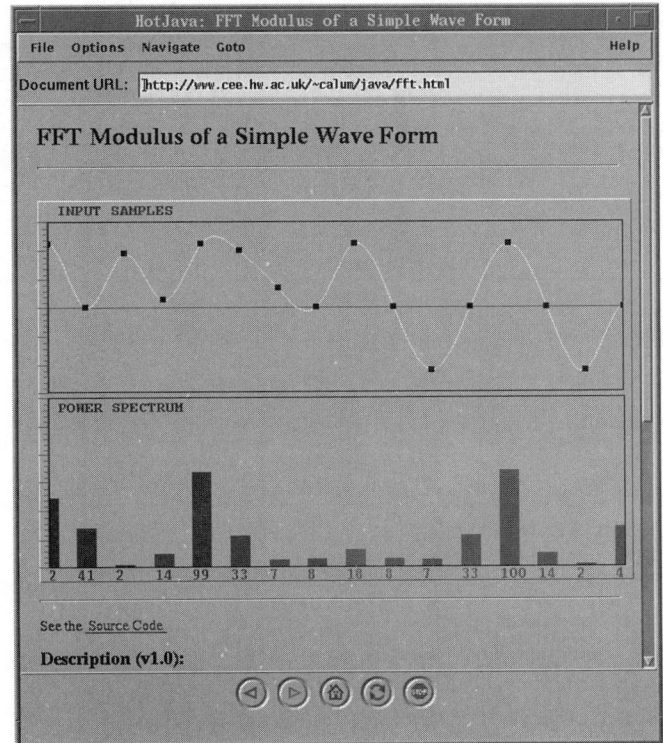

Phasor Demonstration

As a research associate at Heriot-Watt University in Scotland, Yuri Rzhanov (http://www.cee.hw.ac.uk/~yuri/index.html) has created various demonstrations of online course information. His Java demonstration of phasors illustrates a basic concept in electrical engineering.

Rzhanov's PhasorApplet is a good example of a general-purpose applet that can be used for many demonstrations. Yuri explains on the applet's page (http://www.cee.hw.ac.uk/~yuri/java/phasor.html) that the applet is meant to be for "interactive illustrations suitable to explain some particular thesis of the lecturer," not as a full environment for students to explore the phenomenon of phasors. Toward that goal, the PhasorApplet supports many attributes to suit the lecturer's needs:

Attribute	Explanation
n = int	number of phasors
on_top = boolean	summation of phasor's show_scale = boolean show numerical scale

Attribute	Explanation
f0 = int	first phasor frequency
f1 = int	second phasor frequency
p0 = int	first phasor initial phase
p1 = int	second phasor initial phase
a0 = int	first phasor initial magnitude a1 = int second phasor initial magnitude

A lecturer can use this applet to create a set of phasors on the same page by including the applet with different settings for the attributes.

For example, here is the HTML code to demonstrate phasors:

```
<P><APP Src = "http://www.cee.hw.ac.uk/~yuri/java/"
     Class = "phasor.PhasorApplet"
     on_top = "false"
     show_scale = "true"
     n      = "2"
     f0     = "5"
     f1     = "15"
     p0     = "45"
     p1     = "135"
     a0     = "15"
     a1     = "5"
     >

<APP Src = "http://www.cee.hw.ac.uk/~yuri/java/"
     Class = "phasor.StripChartApplet"
     on_top = "false"
     show_scale = "true"
     n      = "2"
     f0     = "5"
     f1     = "15"
     p0     = "45"
     p1     = "135"
     a0     = "15"
     a1     = "5"
     >
```

Figure 5.8 shows a demonstration of these example settings.

When the user moves the cursor over the Press to Run button and holds down the mouse button, the phasors rotate with their given speed in the PhasorApplet on the left. In the StripChartApplet on the right, the chart shows the trace of the tips of the phasors as they rotate. The chart shows how the short phasor is rotating three times faster than the longer one (a frequency of 15 versus a frequency of 5).

Figure 5.8.
Phasor Demonstration.
(Courtesy of Yuri
Rzhanov)

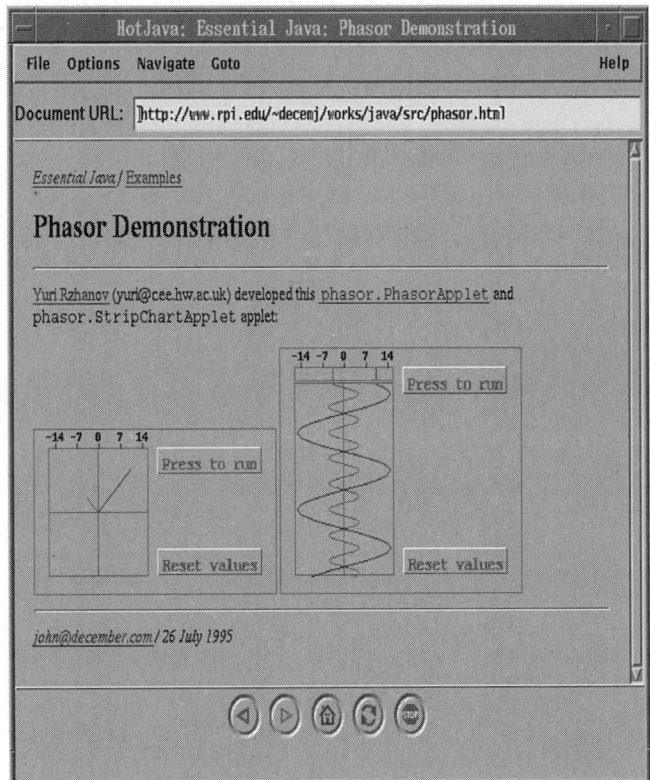

Chapter Summary

Java not only brings animation to Web pages, but it enables users to interact with those anima-tions. Ranging from applets that implement Web-based versions of familiar games to new kinds of Java programs that help users learn, Java interactivity has much potential. Because Java is still in its infancy, the key to developing more complex Java programs will be quality class li-braries. These libraries should help Java programmers express the unique features of an applet without having to worry about coding all the details.

- A simple Hang Duke game demonstrates how user input through the keyboard can affect a graphical display.
- A video poker game adds the element of chance and a tactile visual metaphor to an applet.

■ An applet demonstrating fractal algorithms can help users gain insight into how an algorithm progresses.

■ A user can interact with an applet by matching a picture with foreign words in a word match game. With a speaker to deliver audio, the resulting applet is a model for a useful instructional tool.

■ The examples of the fast fourier transform and the phasor applets show how a Java Web page can become an adjunct to laboratory work. The applets can behave like scientific instruments or interpret and display input data so that students can focus on the meaning of scientific principles.

CHAPTER 6

Java Distributes Content

Because Java is designed for distributing executable content, *all* Java applets, except those on the user's local host, are distributed across networks. However, Java's power as a language for expressing executable content involves more than the distribution of applets. Java also makes the following possible:

- Protocol handlers that communicate to a Java-enabled browser how to handle a new method of processing information.
- Content handlers that give a Java-enabled browser the capability to interpret new data formats.
- Java language statements to access network resources. This enables Java programs to retrieve resources in a user's Java-enabled browser.

This chapter examines these capabilities in detail, showing examples and key Java statements that make these features possible. Part IV of this book guides you through some of Java's programming basics.

The Significance of Network Distribution and Retrieval

Chapter 4 showed an applet (Magic) that allowed you to draw on images (refer to figure 4.5). The network relationships involved in this simple applet are fairly significant. Figure 6.1 shows the relationships of the content distribution, retrieval, and display involved in this applet.

Figure 6.1.
*Summary of informa-
tion transfer in Magic
applet demonstration.*

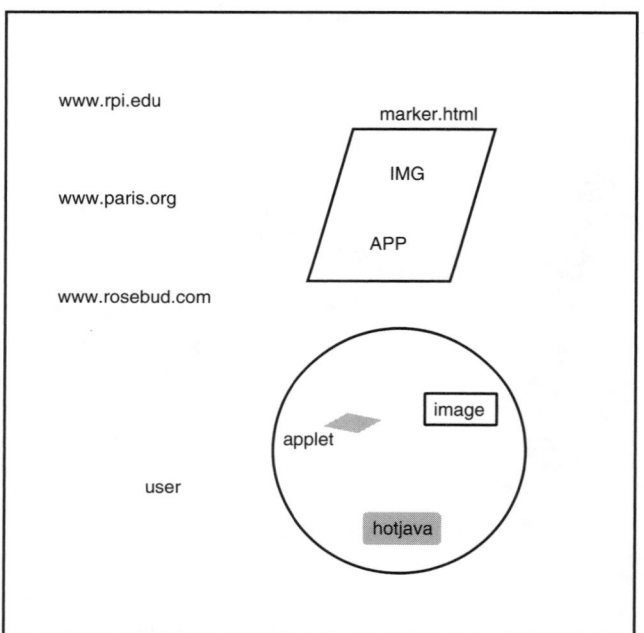

The figure shows the network retrieval taking place:

■ The Web server www.rpi.edu sends the hypertext file marker.html to the user's HotJava browser.

■ The IMG and APP elements in marker.html cause the HotJava browser to request an image from the Web server www.paris.org and an applet from www.rosebud.com.

■ The resulting image, applet, and hypertext page are assembled in the user's HotJava browser. The applet executes on the user's computer.

This network interaction involves three Web servers and the user's computer, besides the routers involved with the Internet network connections that relay the information from two continents. This intermingling of content demonstrates the integration Java can help accomplish.

As a Web client, a Java-enabled browser is already an information integrator for many protocols. Combined with capabilities to distribute and retrieve content, Java adds another dimension to information retrieval and integration.

Handling New Protocols and Formats

The most significant feature of a Java-enabled browser is that it is not fixed (see Chapter 8). Instead of relying on a built-in set of code for handling information delivery protocols and a fixed set of helper applications to handle media formats, a Java-enabled browser is set up so that it can adjust to learn new protocols and media formats.

This capability significantly changes the Web:

■ Developers no longer have to rely on just the fixed set of protocols.

■ Java-enabled browsers can respond to new protocols. These protocols may support new applications or may be new kinds of protocols for information transfer.

Protocol Handlers

A protocol handler is a Java class written, compiled, and placed in a particular part of the browser's directory structure. A programmer creates a protocol handler to devise a new way of interpreting content. A new protocol makes it possible to have a new keyword at the start of a URL. This example shows you how to create a new protocol named run, which runs an applet. This is based on the lesson on protocol handlers that Sun Microsystems provides at http:// java.sun.com/progGuide/getStarted/protocol/index.html.

Here are the essential points of this lesson for creating a new protocol handler called run. First, you write the protocol handler in Java and place it in a file named Handler.java:

```
package net.www.protocol.run;
import java.io.*;
import net.www.html.*;
/**
 *
 * Given a URL of the form
 *          run:classname
 * run a compiled java class
 * Currently the class must be in the CLASSPATH.
 */

class Handler extends URLStreamHandler {
    public synchronized InputStream openStream(URL u) {
        PipedOutputStream ps = new PipedOutputStream();
        PipedInputStream is = new PipedInputStream(ps);
        PrintStream os = new PrintStream(ps);

        String className = u.file;
        String args;
        className = className.substring(className.lastIndexOf("/") + 1);
        if (className.indexOf("?") != 0) {
```

```
                        className.replace(':', ' ');
            }
            u.setType(URL.content_html);
            os.println("");
            os.print("");
            os.print("
\n\n");
            os.close();
            return is;
        }
}
```

■ This example protocol handler is a subclass of `URLStreamHandler`, so its declaration is

  `class Handler extends URLStreamHandler`

  The class `URLStreamHandler` is part of the Application Programming Interface (API), the set of classes that Java programmers can use to write Java applications and applets.

■ Next, you need to compile this protocol handler code using `javac`, just like any other class. Then, you must place the `Handler.class` file in the `net`/`www`/`protocol` subdirectory in your classes subdirectory. Create the subdirectories `net`, `www`, `protocol`, if necessary.

■ You'll need to tell the browser to look in the `CLASSPATH` variable for the location of these classes to run. (Classes on remote servers will *not* run with this preliminary version of `run`.) In UNIX, you can set the `CLASSPATH` variable like this:

  `$ setenv CLASSPATH pathname-of-class-file-directory`

■ Next, you have to restart the browser in order to read its new value.

Bug in Alpha HotJava

There is a bug in the alpha release of HotJava that won't let the browser recognize changes you've made to applets if you restart HotJava in the classes subdirectory. Check to see the latest on this bug at the Sun Microsystems site at `http://java.sun.com/`.

■ Now your HotJava browser should recognize URLs of the form

  `run:AppletName`

  where *AppletName* is the name of an applet in the class file directory defined in the `CLASSPATH` environment variable. Figure 6.2 shows the results of `run:HelloWorld`.

Figure 6.2.
A simple demonstration of a protocol handler.

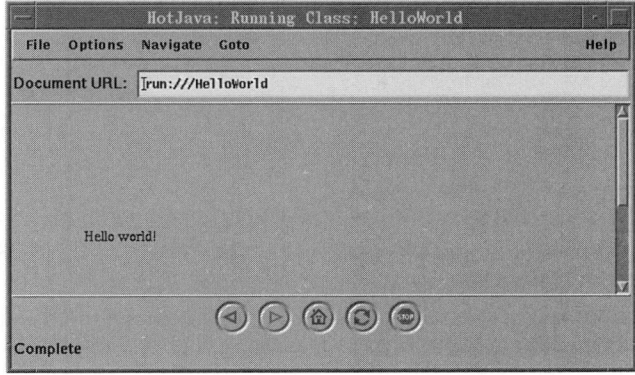

Content Handlers

Like protocol handlers, content handlers also enable a HotJava browser to interpret a new format for information delivery. A content handler translates a particular specification for a file type based on Multipurpose Internet Mail Extensions (MIME) for the HotJava browser.

Sun provides a good online lesson on content handlers at `http://java.sun.com/progGuide/ getStarted/content/index.html`.

Here is the code for the content handler class from that example. You write and compile this code in a file named `plain.java`:

```
/*
 * Plain text file handler
 */
package net.www.content.text;
import net.www.html.ContentHandler;
import net.www.html.URL;
import java.io.InputStream;
import awt.GifImage;

public class plain extends ContentHandler {
    public Object getContent(InputStream is, URL u) {
        StringBuffer sb = new StringBuffer();
        int c;

        while ((c = is.read()) >= 0) {
            sb.appendChar((char)c);
        }
        sb.append("\n\n--and may I add that you look lovely today.\n");
        is.close();
        return sb.toString();
    }
}
```

This code is a very simple demonstration; it echoes the contents of a file of the plain/text type to the browser display and appends a message on the end, --and may I add that you look lovely today.

The essential points for creating a new protocol handler for file types plain/text are

- The source code for plain.java includes its identification as a package:

  package net.www.content.text;

- The file type for the content handler interprets must be a MIME subtype. See Appendix B for a table of MIME types.

- You compile the Java code plain.java and place the plain.class file in a special subdirectory in the classes directory corresponding to the MIME type: net/www/content/text.

- In order to find the content handler, the browser has to be informed to look in the CLASSPATH variable for the location of the classes directory.

- You can configure a file named .mailcap to handle special MIME types. If you have already entered a line in .mailcap that handles the type plain/text, you should remove or comment out that line so that the HotJava browser can handle the type. (The HotJava browser, then, and not a helper application as may have been defined in the .mailcap file, now handles the type.) If you've not created a .mailcap file, you can skip this step.

- You can then use this content handler to interpret *any* file on any host that has the file extension .text. For example, figure 6.3 shows HotJava's interpretation of http://www.rpi.edu/~decemj/works/java/src/test.text.

Figure 6.3.
A simple demonstration of content handler.

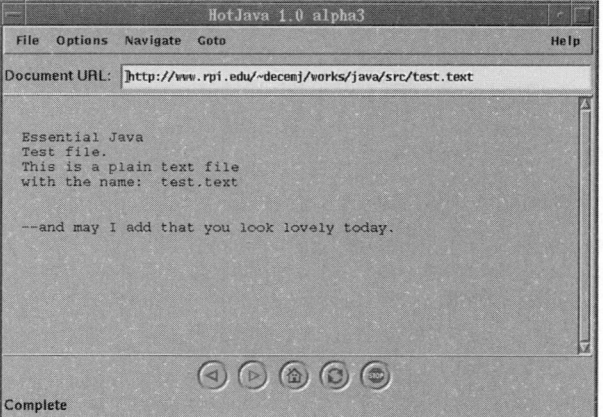

Retrieving Network Information

The protocol and content handlers can expand what a Java-enabled browser can interpret and display, opening the Web for delivery of diverse information. Java also has the capability to enrich how browsers retrieve information, giving Java programmers the chance to make applets to retrieve network information.

Surf-o-matic

Patrick Chan, writing about his Surf-o-matic demonstration program at `http://java.sun.com/applets/applets/autopilot/index.html`, calls it "almost as good as watching TV!" Surf-o-matic is a Web tour guide that can "take over" a user's browser and change the pages. This type of tour has great potential for advertising, education, and other applications.

Surf-o-matic is a Java applet that uses a set of classes to implement the Surf-o-matic Control Panel (figure 6.4). This control panel allows you to cruise the Web based on some lists of "random" URLs. First, you select which list or lists of URLs you want to surf. Then click on the Go button on the panel, and Surf-o-matic takes over your browser. Surf-o-matic switches the page every 20 seconds (or a time interval you can set) to a new page from the random lists you've chosen. Yahoo's (`http://www.yahoo.com/`) random list of Web pages is very large and is used in the example in figure 6.4.

Figure 6.4.
Surf-o-matic in action.
(Courtesy of Patrick
Chan, Sun
Microsystems)

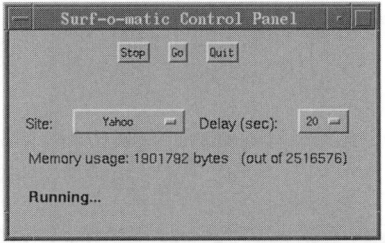

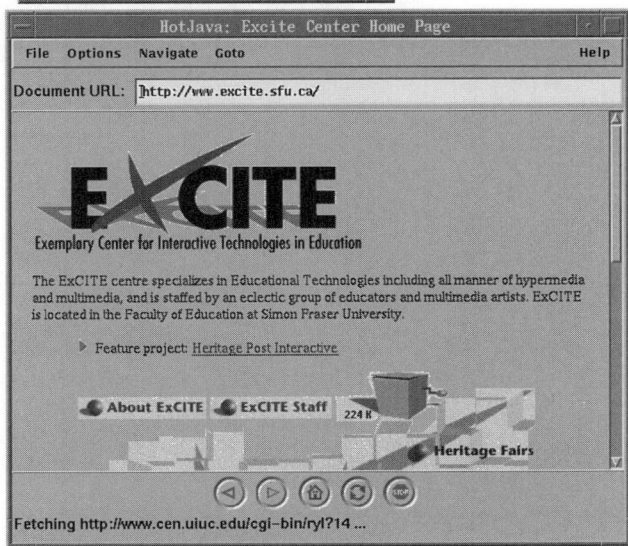

Figure 6.4 shows Surf-o-matic as it is retrieving a new page. Even in its present form, it is a useful standalone application. One use is as a kiosk application to demonstrate the content of the Web.

Surf-o-matic is based on Matthew Gray's Web Autopilot, which uses the Netscape browser's client-pull feature. However, a HotJava browser can use Java code to implement this same type of task; it then does not have to revert to a client-pull technique. Patrick Chan's demonstration in Surf-o-matic is a quick example showing this flexibility of Java for network information retrieval.

VPRO Tour Guide

A public broadcasting organization in The Netherlands, VPRO (`http://www.vpro.nl/`), has created a tour guide similar in spirit to Surf-o-matic. Figure 6.5 shows the VPRO tour guide, at `http://www.vpro.nl/htbin/scan/www/interaktief/java/control.html`, in operation.

Figure 6.5.
The VPRO guided tour.
(Courtesy of Daniel
Ockeloen, VPRO, The
Netherlands)

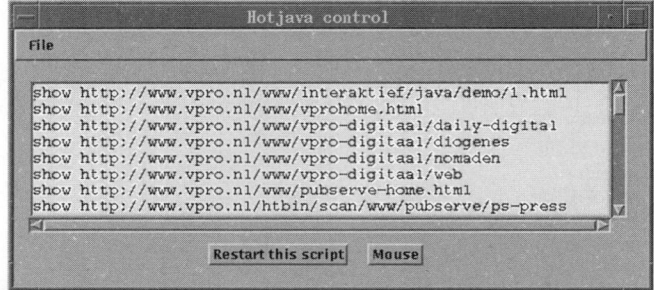

The guide takes you through a tour of Web pages on the VRPO site. Unlike in Surf-o-matic, this tour is not random, but is based on a carefully selected sequence of URLs. The list of URLs is shown in the example session in figure 6.5, in the HotJava control panel.

Both Surf-o-matic and the VPRO Tour Guide offer their source code from their sites (at the URLs shown here) so that programmers can understand how to accomplish this network retrieval. The Java programmer can use the Java classes `net.www.html.*`, which are part of the Java API. These classes are in the `classes/net/www/html/` directory of the Java code distribution. The classes in `classes/browser/` can also be used for interface objects.

One key programming line in Surf-o-matic is the actual pushing of the URL. With the object document declared as type `WRWindow` (a class in `classes/browser`), this line brings up the new URL:

```
document.pushURL(siteMenu.getURL());
```

The VPRO tour guide uses a technique of creating a reference to an object, browser of type `hotjava`:

```
hotjava browser;
```

and then using the go method to change the browser to a string identifying a URL, `nextUrl`:

```
browser.go(nextUrl);
```

Surf-o-matic and the VRPO tour guide each bring a new dimension to the Web: a Java-enabled browser can retrieve more Web pages for the user in a particular sequence. Used creatively, authors can prepare Web scripts consisting of page sequences on Web servers. Such guided tours may seem to go against the user-centered interactivity that Java makes possible, turning the Web into a sort of slide show or television to passively watch. However, the full potential of Java is still far from realized. These examples are demonstrations and experiments with the technology—experiments with as-yet-unrealized meaning. The potential of Java is clear: the ability to deliver executable content; to react to user choices with continuous, immediate feedback; and to take the user on a tour of Web pages.

Chapter Summary

Java not only changes what can happen on a Web page, it also changes what can be retrieved and displayed on a Web page. Special handlers for new protocols and content extend what a HotJava browser can find and interpret.

- A protocol handler is written as a class, compiled, and placed in a directory corresponding to its protocol type.
- A content handler also is a class, specifically written to specify how a HotJava browser should handle a MIME data type.
- Java enables network information retrieval within applets, making it possible for an applet to take over a user's display and exhibit a series of network resources.

Using the HotJava Browser

The Java programming language provides opportunities for creating rich ways of communicating on the Web. The Java language, however, requires a Web special browser to observe it.

Pre-Java browsers will not display Java content, so you have to get a Java-enabled browser to observe Java programs. If your Web browser isn't Java enabled, it will ignore the APP tag that identifies an applet and not display Java content. The HotJava browser was created (programmed in the Java language itself) to demonstrate Java's capabilities, and it is available free for noncommercial use.

Available initially for a few platforms, HotJava is now being ported to more platforms. More commercial browsers are expected to integrate Java technology into future releases.

The chapters in this part examine the HotJava browser in detail, showing how to check for its most current releases, download, unpack, and use them. Chapter 7 describes the releases available as of this writing and gives directions for finding other Java-enabled browsers. Chapter 8 examines the HotJava browser in detail and highlights how it differs in operation and design from previous generations of browsers. Chapter 9 reviews how HotJava also functions similarly—from the user's viewpoint—to previous Web browsers.

These chapters give you:

- An explanation of the HotJava browser and how to check for, download, and unpack the latest releases
- An understanding of how HotJava is a browser with a built-in capability to learn more protocols and data formats; it does not need to rely on a fixed set of built-in protocols
- Knowledge of how to use HotJava's interface for navigating the Web

CHAPTER 7

HotJava is a Web Browser for Java

As you saw from Parts I and II of this book, Java is a programming language designed to deliver executable content across networks. If you want to view or interact with Java executable content, you must have a Java-enabled browser that can interpret the bytecodes created from Java language files. (Chapter 2 reviews the technical design of the Java language and the relationship of the Java code files to the bytecode files.)

This chapter provides a description of what is necessary for you to obtain, download, and install Sun Microsystem's HotJava browser. This chapter also gives references to online sources for the latest information about other Java-enabled browsers.

Java/HotJava Availability

HotJava is a browser from Sun Microsystems that enables the display of interactive content on the Web. Because HotJava is written entirely in Java, it demonstrates the capabilities of the Java programming language.

HotJava is available for use directly from the Sun Microsystems site at http://java.sun.com/. Check at that site for the latest on the licensing terms for HotJava.

The capability to display Java's interactive content is expected to be integrated into many commercial browsers and online services. For the latest information, check the Java page at Sun or the lists of further Web reference information given in Appendix A. You can also use Web search techniques and resources to find the latest offerings for browsers that support Java applets.

The Purpose of HotJava

HotJava is a Web browser, but it also has the capability to interpret executable content. The general scenario is this:

1. Developers write Java source code on their computers.
2. Developers compile the source code using the Java compiler.
3. The result of compilation is an architecture-neutral file of bytecodes.
4. If you have a computer that can support a Java-enabled browser (such as HotJava), you can download and run these bytecodes.

As described in Chapter 2, the architecture-neutral nature of Java is one of its key characteristics. This characteristic, however, means that the Java-enabled browser must be able to interpret these bytecodes (which are architecture-neutral) for the architecture of the user's machine.

The Purpose of Porting

The term *platform* identifies the type of hardware, operating system, or user interface. Programmers have to customize software so that it can run on a particular platform because each platform has different characteristics and the software has to conform to these characteristics. For example, Microsoft's Word is available for personal computers running Windows. The programmers who created Word also made a version for Macintosh computers. This process of customizing software so that it runs on a particular platform is called *porting*. The HotJava browser must be ported to a variety of platforms—as must other Web browsers. The Netscape browser, for example, has a version for the X Window System, another for Windows, and another for the Macintosh.

Figure 7.1 shows the general scheme: the information provider distributes bytecodes to users who may have many different kinds of computers. The ported code for Java creates a "socket" that is customized to the user's platform. The generic bytecodes can "fit" into this ported socket, allowing bytecodes, which are not specific to any platform, to be distributed. Thus, the information provider need not worry about the specifics of the user's platform. Thus, the executable content that Java makes possible is architecture-neutral. The versions of the Java-enabled browser that are specifically written for different platforms make this possible.

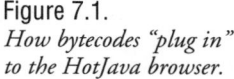

Figure 7.1.
How bytecodes "plug in" to the HotJava browser.

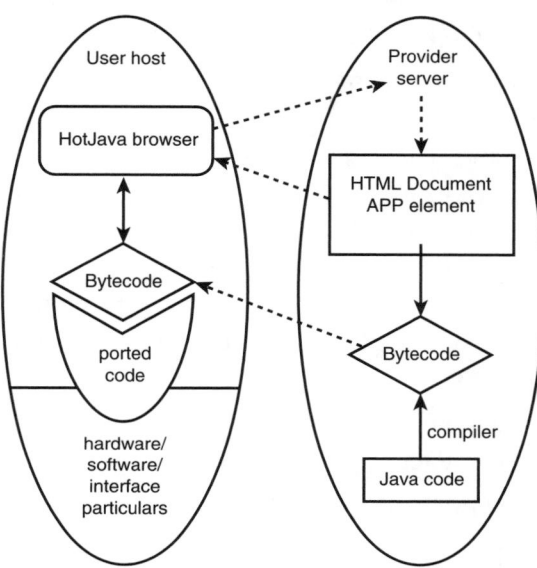

Java Ports Completed

In the summer of 1995, development was completed at Sun Microsystems for HotJava (alpha release) for

- Sun Solaris 2.3, 2.4, and 2.5 SPARC-based machines.

  Solaris is Sun Microsystem's software platform for networked applications. Solaris includes an operating system, SunOS. For more information on Solaris, see `http://www.sun.com/cgi-bin/show?sunsoft/solaris/index.body`.

  SPARC stands for Scalable Processor ARChitecture. SPARC is a technology developed by Sun Microsystems and others. It is based on a reduced instruction set computer (RISC) concept in which a microprocessor is designed for very efficient handling of a small set of instructions. For more information, see `http://www.sparc.com/`.

- Intel x86 machines with Windows NT 3.5.

  "Intel x86" means computers that use the Intel family of "86" microprocessors. This includes the Intel 286, 386, 486, or Pentium processors. For more information, see `http://www.intel.com/`.

  Windows NT is Microsoft's operating system for the Internet. For more information, see `http://www.microsoft.com/`.

Ports Underway

Development was underway (summer 1995) at Sun Microsystems for porting HotJava to the following platforms:

- Microsoft Windows 95.

  Windows 95 is Microsoft's next generation of user interface software for personal computers, released in August 1995. For more information, see `http://www.microsoft.com/`.

- Macintosh operating system 7.5. (See `http://www.apple.com/`.)

In the summer of 1995, developers outside Sun Microsystems were working on ports of HotJava to these platforms:

- Amiga computer. (See `http://www.yahoo.com/Computers/PCs/Amiga/`.)
- NeXT computer. (See `http://www.next.com/`.)
- Linux operating system.

  Linux is a UNIX-like operating system written by Linus Torvalds with assistance from a team of others on the Net. It runs on 386/486-based PCs. For more information, see `http://www.yahoo.com/Computers/Operating_Systems/Unix/Linux/`.

- Netscape Communications plans to integrate Java technology into its browser; for the latest information, check Netscape's site at `http://home.netscape.com/`.

Online Java Installation Information

Sun Microsystem's Java site (`http://java.sun.com/`) is the best place to look for the latest online information about obtaining HotJava. In particular,

`http://java.sun.com/installation.html`	Describes the current sites and instructions for downloading HotJava.
`http://java.sun.com/source.html`	Describes information about the latest release of Java.
`http://java.sun.com/porting.html`	Describes the latest in porting efforts.
`http://java.sun.com/bugsandfeatures.html`	Check this for the latest on problems or requested features.

Downloading and Using HotJava

Downloading and installation procedures will vary based on the platform you have. This section shows the download procedures for UNIX as a model to give you a general idea of what is involved in downloading, installing, and running HotJava.

Both the source and binary releases of Java/HotJava are available. The source release includes the code used to implement Java/HotJava and is available from Sun by special request (see Sun's Java site at the URL given in the box). Only those wanting to know how Java works in detail or who are interested in writing a HotJava port to another platform would need to obtain the source code. The source code for HotJava is written in the Java language itself, as HotJava is an application of the Java language.

First Step: Find Out If There is a Port to Your Platform

The binary release is what a typical user of Java/HotJava should obtain. A binary release is one that includes an executable file ready to run on the user's platform. The first step is to find out if a port of Java has been completed for your platform. Use the URL `http://java.sun.com/porting.html` to check for this. If a port has been completed for your platform, you'll need to know how to obtain it. Usually, these are distributed through File Transfer Protocol (FTP) sites or through Web sites. You'll need the URL of the site for downloading for the next step.

If you have a UNIX platform, you can find its characteristics by using the `uname` command. This command displays the name of the current system and other information. The key pieces of information to check are available as options of this command: The `-s` option displays the operating system name, the `-r` option displays the operating system release, and the `-p` option displays the processor type. (The `-a` option displays all available information.) This example shows the `uname` command used to identify the user's platform:

```
$ /usr/bin/uname -srp
SunOS 5.4 sparc
```

This response is good because Java (in alpha) release has been ported to SPARC-based machines. If the processor name doesn't correspond to a system for which a port has been completed, the browser will *not* run on the system.

Second Step: Downloading

After you have the URL of the site where HotJava is available, the next step is downloading. The examples shown in this section show typical procedures for downloading HotJava for a UNIX and a PC platform.

It is important that you respect the intellectual property protection on the Java/HotJava source code. The source code is not public domain and requires a license for redistribution. However, writing applets and distributing them does not require a license. For the definitive, final word on the legal terms and conditions for the source code or binaries for HotJava, see the statements provided by Sun Microsystems (or licensees) in the binary or source distribution itself.

Sun Microsystems provides a main site and some mirror sites (sites that contain duplicates of the distribution code) for downloading Java/HotJava. These sites offer access to the code through anonymous file transfer protocol (FTP). These sites include:

- Anonymous FTP to `java.sun.com` (the main Java/Hot Java FTP server operated by Sun Microsystems). If you already have a Web browser, you can access Sun's Java site at `http://java.sun.com` to download HotJava.
- SunSITEs (Sun Information and Technology Exchange) worldwide. Anonymous FTP to `sunsite.unc.edu`, directory `/pub/sun-info/hotjava/`.
- SunSITEs are sponsored by Sun Microsystems at universities around the world. For a list of SunSITEs, which may carry Java/HotJava distributions, see `http://www.sun.com/sunsite/`.

The alpha release of HotJava for UNIX also requires the graphical interface OpenWindows version 3.0 or above. UNIX workstations commonly have a variant of X Window System installed. For more information on the X Window System, see the X Consortium at `http://www.x.org/`.

You should next be sure that enough diskspace is available for the download. The alpha version of uncompressed Java/HotJava required approximately 10 MB, so this is a likely minimum for the total amount of diskspace needed. The online downloading instructions will tell you how much diskspace is required for your machine.

If you already have a Web browser, you can use it to locate the distribution and download it. Sun's downloading instructions give you links that you can click on to do the download.

If you don't have a Web browser, you can obtain HotJava via anonymous FTP. The following example shows an example session for UNIX, with user inputs shown in **bold**. This example shows you how to look in the distribution directory for the latest release version and number. You can then use the `mget` command to quickly request the filenames to download.

```
$ ftp java.sun.com
Connected to java.sun.com.
220 java FTP server (Version wu-2.4(3) Wed Feb 15 15:57:20 PST 1995) ready.
Name (java.sun.com:john): anonymous
331 Guest login ok, send your complete e-mail address as password.
Password: enter your email address here
230-Welcome to the Java/HotJava ftp server.
230-
230-Information about your login and any transfers you do are
230-logged on this host. If you disagree with this policy
230-please disconnect now.
230-
230-Information about this service may be obtained by browsing
230-
230-    http://java.sun.com/
230-
230-Please contact csw@sun.com with any technical problems you have
230-with this server.
230-
230-You are user 116 out of a maximum of 150 users.
230-It is Mon Jul 10 17:39:48 1995 in Palo Alto, Ca.
230-
230 Guest login ok, access restrictions apply.
ftp> cd pub
```

```
250-STOP! STOP! STOP! STOP! STOP! STOP! STOP! STOP! STOP! STOP! STOP!
250-====================================================================
[informational message about the latest version compatibility]
ftp> binary
200 Type set to I.
ftp> ls
200 PORT command successful.
150 Opening ASCII mode data connection for file list.
java
images
.message
.history.java
starwave
OLD
.orig
hotjava-alpha3-solaris2-sparc.tar.Z
sb_nt.exe
unz512xN.exe
hotjava-alpha2-nt-x86.exe
226 Transfer complete.
150 bytes received in 0.0068 seconds (22 Kbytes/s)
ftp> mget hotjava*
mget hotjava-alpha2-nt-x86.exe? no
mget hotjava-alpha3-solaris2-sparc.tar.Z? yes
200 PORT command successful.
150 Opening BINARY mode data connection for hotjava-alpha3-solaris2-sparc.tar.Z
(5476531 bytes).
ftp> quit
```

Notice that in these instructions, you simply respond "yes" to the version for your platform. After this transfer is completed, you are ready for the next step: unpacking.

Step Three: Unpacking

Once downloaded, the binary file can be uncompressed and unpacked with the UNIX command:

```
zcat hotjava-alpha3-solaris2-sparc.tar.Z | tar xf -
```

This will create a subdirectory called hotjava/ in the current directory. Once this has been done, the original file ending with tar.Z is no longer needed and can be deleted to save diskspace on your machine.

Step Four: Seeing What You Have

Once HotJava is unpacked, you'll have a set of files and directories in the hotjava sudirectory. These include

README	A general information file describing the release and latest information about it.
bin	The directory of binaries for the HotJava browser and related Java language tools.

classes	Directories of the bytecodes for classes in the Java distribution (files ending with .class). These include (for alpha release):

	awt	A package of classes for handling windows and graphical features.
	browser	Classes that make up HotJava. (Remember, the HotJava browser is a Java application, written in Java.)
	java	Classes that make up the support for the Java language, such as input/output, utilities, and tools.
	net	Classes that support network communication, including protocols such as for news, mail, FTP, and Web-related protocols such as HTTP.

classsrc	Directories of the Java language source code for classes in the Java distribution (files ending with .java). Note that this isn't the Java "source" described previously (which implements the Java language), but the source code for the Java distribution classes, including the Java source code for the HotJava browser.
copyright.html	Read this file for the definitive statement on intellectual property protection and appropriate use for the Java distribution.
demo	A set of Java demonstration programs.
doc	The complete set of documents, in HTML, to support Java. Includes source files for online documents viewable through HotJava.
include	Header files in Java programming.
index.html	An index into user information provided in the distribution; this is the default page that appears in the HotJava browser when it is started.
lib	These are the library files used in Java programming.
readme.html	HTML version of introductory information.

Step Five: Running HotJava

The bin directory contains the binary for the HotJava browser as well as the other tools distributed (including the Java language interpreter and compiler). You can run HotJava by changing to this directory and entering the command hotjava &. (The & sign after the program name "forks" the process so you can have the browser run while more commands can be entered at the UNIX prompt). Here is an example of going into the unpacked directory and running HotJava:

```
$ cd hotjava
$ ls
README     classsrc    doc        lib
bin        copyright.html include   readme.html
```

```
classes      demo       index.html
$ cd bin
$ ls
hotjava      javac      javah      javap_g
java         javac_g    javah_g    javaprof
java_g       javadoc    javap      sun4
$ hotjava &
```

Other Software That Comes with HotJava

If you've downloaded the HotJava browser, you've also obtained the software tools necessary to develop Java applications. These are summarized and some are demonstrated in more detail in Chapter 2, and all are documented in the manual pages that come with the Java distribution (in the directory `hotjava/doc/man/`). Part IV of this book shows how you can use these tools to create Java applets and applications. These tools include:

- Java compiler `javac`, which translates the human-readable Java source code to machine-readable bytecodes.
- Java interpreter `java`, which executes Java programs.
- C header and source file generator `javah`, `javah_g`. This generates C header and source files for making methods.
- Java disassembler `javap`, which prints out information about a class file.
- Document generator `javadoc`. This can generate an HTML file given a source file.
- Profiling tool`javaprof`. This formats the performance data created by the `-prof` option of the Java interpreter, `java`.

HotJava for Windows NT 3.5

A port for HotJava to Intel x86 machines running Windows NT 3.5 was also available in the alpha version in the summer of 1995. A Windows 95 port was not complete, but is in development at Sun Microsystems.

Downloading Java/HotJava for a Windows distribution via FTP is the same as previously shown for the UNIX version, except the user can respond "yes" when asked for the appropriate file:

```
$ ftp java.sun.com
Connected to java.sun.com.
Name (java.sun.com:john): anonymous
Password: enter your email address here
ftp> binary
ftp> mget hotjava*
mget hotjava-alpha2-nt-x86.exe? yes
ftp> quit
```

Once downloaded, you can unpack the browser by typing the name of the executable at the operating system prompt:

```
c:\ hotjava-xxxx-nt-x86.exe
```

This command runs a self-extracting archive program that will unpack the files and directories.

Similar to running HotJava in UNIX, you can run HotJava in DOS by entering the executable filename at the operating system prompt:

```
c:\hotjava\bin\hotjava
```

Note that you'll need to use the Program Manager in Windows 95 to install HotJava as a new program item.

Chapter Summary

This chapter showed the basic steps to obtain the Java/HotJava browser for noncommercial use. If you want HotJava, the first step is to determine whether a port has been completed for your platform. Second, download the binary source files. If you already have a Web browser, you can click on the links provided on the HotJava distribution page to download. Third, unpack the binary file you downloaded. On UNIX, you can use the zcat command. In DOS, the binary file downloaded is a self-extracting archive. Finally, you run HotJava by entering the name of the executable (hotjava) at the operating system prompt.

- The Java/HotJava distribution is available for noncommercial use and download at ftp://java.sun.com/ or http://java.sun.com/.
- Downloading, unpacking, and running HotJava requires some knowledge of your platform's operating system and file structure.

CHAPTER 8

HotJava is a New Kind of Web Browser

The Java programming language marks a significant advance for interactivity on the Web, and the HotJava browser that showcases Java marks the start of a new generation of smart browsers for the Web. Not constrained to a fixed set of functionality, the HotJava browser can adjust and learn new protocols and formats dynamically. Developers of Web information using Java need no longer be constrained to the text, graphics, and relatively low-quality multimedia of the fixed set available for Web browsers in the pre-Java age. Instead, the HotJava browser opens new possibilities for new protocols and new media formats never before seen on the Web.

This chapter presents a brief survey of how HotJava is significantly and dramatically different than Web browsers that have come before it. The next chapter surveys the operation of HotJava in detail, along with tips on using HotJava to navigate the Web. (Chapter 7 describes how to obtain, download, and install HotJava.)

Java Marks a New Age in Browsers

Through the past half-decade of development of the World Wide Web, new browser technologies have often altered the common view of what the Web and online communication could be. When the Mosaic browser was released in 1993, it rocketed the Web to the attention of the general public because of the graphical, seamless appearance it gave to the Web. Instead of a disparate set of tools to access a variety of information spaces, Mosaic dramatically and visually integrated Internet information. Its point-and-click operation changed ideas about what a Web browser could be, and its immediate successor, Netscape, has likewise grown in popularity and continued to push the bounds of what is presented on the Web.

HotJava, however, marks a very new stage of technological evolution of browsers. HotJava breaks the model of Web browsers as only filters for displaying network information; rather, a Java-age browser acts more like an intelligent interpreter of executable content and a displayer for new protocol and media formats.

Pre-Java Browsers

The earliest browser of the Web was the line mode browser from CERN. The subsequent Mosaic-class browsers (Mosaic and Netscape from 1993 to mid-1995) dramatically opened the graphical view of the Web. However, the Mosaic-type browsers acted as an information filter to Internet-based information. Encoded into these browsers was knowledge of the fundamental Internet protocols and media formats (such as HTTP, NNTP, Gopher, FTP, HTML, and GIF). The browsers matched this knowledge with the protocols and media formats found on the Net, and then displayed the results. Figure 8.1 illustrates this operation as the browser finds material on the Net and interprets it according to its internal programming for protocols or common media formats. These browsers also used helper applications to display specialized media formats such as movies or sound.

A pre-Java browser was very knowledgeable about the common protocols and media formats about the network (and therefore very "bulky"). Unfortunately, a pre-Java browser could not handle protocols for which it had not been programmed or media formats for which it did not have a helper application available. These are the technical shortcomings that a Java-age browser addresses.

Figure 8.1.
Pre-Java browsers acted as filters.

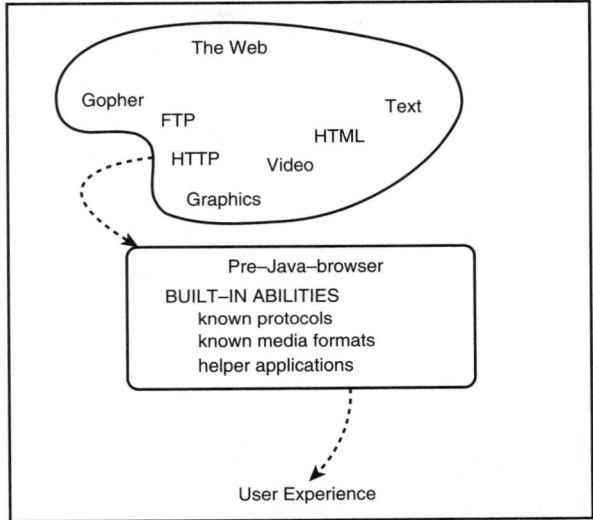

Java-Age Browsers

A Java-age browser is very lightweight because it actually has no *pre-defined protocols* or *media formats* programmed into its core functionality; instead, the core functionality of a HotJava browser consists of the ability to learn how to interpret any protocol or media format. Of course, the HotJava browser is told about the most common protocols and formats as part of its distribution package. In addition, any new format or protocol that a Java programmer might devise, a HotJava browser can learn.

As figure 8.2 shows, a Java-age browser is "lightweight," not coming with a monolithic store of knowledge of the Web, but with the most important ability of all—the ability to learn.

Figure 8.2.
*The Java-age browser
can learn.*

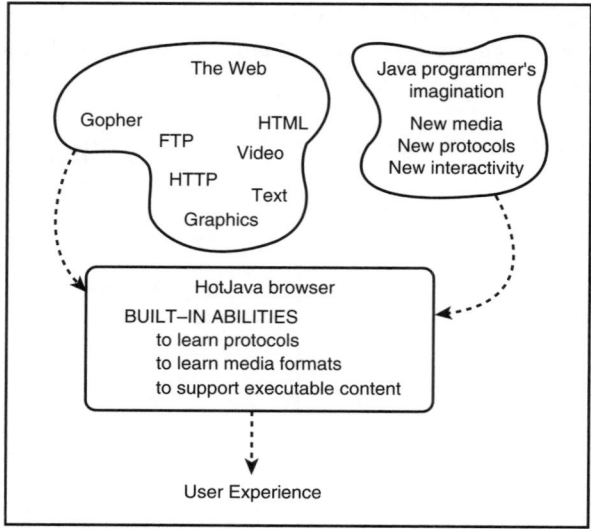

HotJava Features

In addition to being designed differently than previous browsers, HotJava is also specifically designed to show off the capabilities of the Java language. Because the HotJava browser is itself an application written in Java, it is no surprise that it complements the language in every feature: executable content, network communication, and information retrieval. HotJava also includes all the standard features expected in a graphical Web browser.

Executable Content

If you are a new user of HotJava, one of its unique features that you'll probably notice immediately is its capability to display executable content. You saw many examples of this in Part II of this book. When you use the HotJava browser to download a page containing an applet, identified with the hypertext markup language APP tag, the bytecode for that applet is downloaded and run on your computer and displayed in your HotJava browser. After this initial download of the applet code, the applet can run indefinitely (for example, the animations shown in Chapter 1 or Chapter 4) without further downloading across the network.

The Java language also supports "multithreaded" applets. This means that there can be several activities or happenings on a single Web page at the same time. This makes it possible for the user to have many things to interact with or watch.

Network Content

HotJava is also designed specifically to distribute content over networks, and therefore includes security considerations to protect the user's computer. HotJava recognizes an environment variable called HOTJAVA_WRITE_PATH, which sets the path of files that any applets may write to.

You can do this in UNIX by setting this variable to a list of files or directories separated by colons. For example:

```
$ setenv HOTJAVA_WRITE_PATH /tmp/:/user/smith/data/:/devices/:~/.hotjava
```

This command will allow the applets to write to files only in the /tmp/ directory and to the directories /user/smith/data/, /devices/, and ~/.hotjava. This last path is in the user's directory (~/.hotjava). This write capability can also be set in the Options/Properties section of the HotJava titlebar.

HotJava supports all of the major Internet information protocols for network communication: HTTP, news, mailto, FTP, and Gopher. For accessing Usenet news, the NNTPSERVER variable can be set to the name of the local NNTP server.

HotJava's Browser Features

The HotJava browser has many of the interface features of a standard Web browser. As a user, you can control some HotJava features, including:

- **Image and applet loading.** You can turn off the automatic loading of images and applets.
- **URL requests.** A user can make a request for a resource by URL in several ways. For example, using File/Open from the titlebar or by entering the URL directly into the Document URL box at the top of the browser.

You also have access to some useful information-managing features in HotJava, including the following:

- **Documentation online.** The HotJava browser presents an interface to documentation through the Help selection from the titlebar.
- **URL hotlist managers.** This includes a history list, a hotlist, and a special kind of quick access list called a "goto" list.

Information developers can use some of the Netscape extensions. HotJava in the alpha version recognizes <CENTER>... </CENTER> to center text. It also recognizes these horizontal rule (<HR>)attributes:

- **Size="number".** How thin the line should be in pixels. Example 1 in figure 8.3 is 15 pixels thick and runs the whole width of the display.
- **Noshade.** Turns off shading to create a solid bar. In Example 2 (figure 8.3) there is a 1-pixel solid bar that runs the whole width of the display.
- **Width="number|percent".** The width of the line, either expressed as width in pixels (number, as in Example 3 is 100 pixels wide) or a relative as a percent of the current display width (not page width). Example 4 is 33% of the display width. These lines are by default centered. (Default can be overridden with the Align attribute.)

■ **Align="left|right|center".** The alignment of horizontal lines that are less than the full width of the page. Example 5 is a 5-pixel bar that is 10% of the display wide and aligned to the right.

The alpha version of HotJava did **not** recognize colored backgrounds, font size changes, the **BLINK** element, or tables.

The next chapter takes you on a tour of how to put these features to use.

Figure 8.3.
HotJava interpretation of Netscape extensions to the attributes of the HR element.

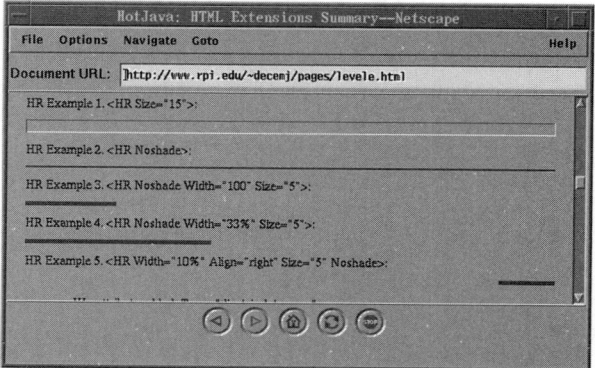

Chapter Summary

This chapter described how the HotJava Web browser differs from and is, in some cases, the same as Web browsers invented before it. HotJava's unique features are its ability to learn new protocols and media formats and display executable content.

■ The HotJava browser demonstrates major new capabilities for Web browsers.

■ HotJava can interpret new protocols and media formats because of its ability to download executable content across networks.

■ HotJava has features for network security and network communications.

■ HotJava has many standard control and display features of a typical graphical Web browser.

CHAPTER 9

You Can Navigate the Web with HotJava

The previous two chapters reviewed how to obtain and download HotJava and how HotJava differs from other Web browsers. HotJava is also similar to other Web browsers in its graphical interface for navigating the Web. This chapter provides you a tour of the HotJava interface, stressing the functional areas of support HotJava provides.

> **Note:** The alpha version of the HotJava browser shown here will change as new versions are developed and released. Also, other browsers that incorporate Java technology will likely provide somewhat different interfaces than HotJava does. However, all versions should provide similar support and functionality as described here.

This chapter begins with a tour of HotJava's user interface to show you how it supports the needs of a Web navigator. The last part of this chapter presents some general tips for finding information on the Web; you can use these tips and techniques to find information on the Web as well as keep current with new Java and other technologies.

The HotJava User Interface

Figure 9.1 shows HotJava displaying its index page. HotJava's user interface, even in its alpha form as shown in the figure, presents a fairly complete set of functions for navigating the Web.

Figure 9.1.

HotJava's index page.

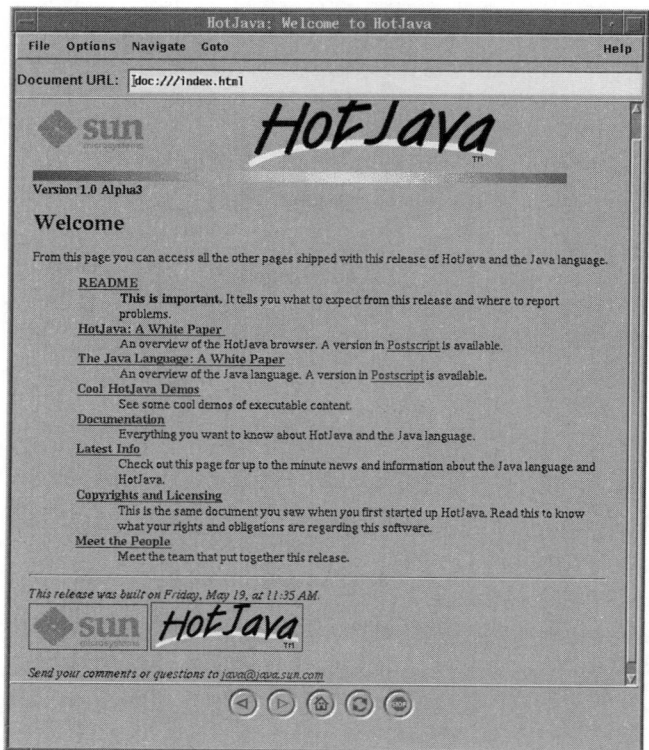

The browser shown in figure 9.1 is the alpha version of HotJava for the X Window system. The figure illustrates the following features.

- The name of the page is shown at the very top of the browser. (The name reads `HotJava: Welcome to HotJava`.)
- Below the name of the page is a titlebar menu of options. These include **File**, **Options**, **Navigate**, and **Goto**.

- The Document URL window displays the URL of the page currently displayed in HotJava. In the figure, this URL is `doc:///index.html`. The prefix of this URL, `doc`, is actually a special protocol for displaying Java documentation.

- The display area, or browser window, is under the window showing the URL page. This area displays the contents of the page.

- At the bottom of the browser are buttons that provide one-button access to popular navigation tasks: backward, forward, home, reload, and stop loading.

How HotJava Helps You Navigate the Web

While navigating the Web, you have a set of needs that may be thought of an existing hierarchy. The most basic needs, for information display, link activation, and movement, form a core set of functionality that any Web browser should offer. Other, higher-level needs are "nice to have" features that many modern graphical browsers implement. This section traces through how the HotJava browser supports this hierarchy of needs for Web navigators. The needs are discussed starting with the most basic ones first and moving up the hierarchy:

1. **Information display.** A visual, aural, or other sensory representation of a Web document or Net information file or service to you. This is the most basic need for a Web navigator because this display is the basis for information transmittal and perception.

2. **Link activation.** The ability to activate a hyperlink so that the browser displays resources to which the link refers. This is key for enabling the Web navigator to select more resources in a hypertext document.

3. **Movement.** The ability to select a link from a set of previously visited resources or to move directly to a particular resource. Movement is key for a Web navigator to make good use of the Web, and it enables a Web navigator to be more flexible in following paths.

4. **Information control.** The ability to control information retrieval and display. This is key for giving you the ability to make choices about stopping or limiting information retrieval.

5. **Interactivity.** The ability for you to transmit specific information (beyond just information about link activation choice) to a Web server or information provider.

6. **Options and feedback.** Features to enable you to be more efficient and customize the Web browser to your preferences.

7. **Web actualization.** A need for a user to become so adept with using the browser that she can seamlessly observe the vast panoply of networked information on the Web.

The following sections examine how HotJava supports each of these needs in detail.

Information Display

HotJava provides graphical features to enable you to read text and graphics, identify hotlinks, and identify any special-case browser symbols.

Text in HotJava, as displayed in figure 9.1, is shown using a scheme that has come to be fairly standard for graphical Web browsers: a default font is used to display all text information in HTML documents, with special fonts used for headings, or when used in HTML character formatting (see Appendix C for a summary of HTML tags). Inline images are displayed as integrated into the text display. HotJava supports scrolling for hypertext pages that go beyond a single screen as displayed in the browser.

Some areas of text and graphics displayed in a browser are linked to other resources, such as Web pages or multimedia files. These links are displayed as underlined and highlighted text in HotJava. Following the convention of previous graphical Web browsers, HotJava shows these links in blue, with a change to a different shade of blue after you select the link.

Special symbols in HotJava cue you about conditions of the information display. These symbols are to indicate the status of image and applet loading:

- A gray box represents an image or applet that is in the process of loading. A graphical image that is still downloading will have a small icon of a portrait in it.
- A yellow box might appear that has a portrait icon in it is displayed instead of an image because you have selected to turn off automatic image loading. You can retrieve this image by clicking on it.
- A yellow box might appear that has a blue upper left corner and a portrait icon. The portrait icon—rather than an image—appears because the image is linked to another resource and you have turned off automatic image loading. You can follow the link by clicking on the blue corner or retrieve the image by clicking on the yellow part of the box.
- A yellow box with a gear icon appears instead of an applet; the applet has not been loaded because you have turned off automatic applet loading. You can retrieve this applet by clicking on the yellow box.
- A red box with a portrait icon in it indicates an error in loading an image.
- A red box with a gear icon in it indicates an error in loading an applet.
- A red box with a blue upper left corner and a portrait icon indicates that an error occurred in loading an image that is linked to another resource.

Link Activation

You can activate links in HotJava by clicking on a hotspot. A hotspot is any part of a Web page that can be linked to some other Web resource. A hotspot can be the words of a hypertext link shown as blue highlighted text or an imagemap, which connects pixels in an inline image to a resource. A hotspot can also be an image linked to another resource. After the hotspot is selected, the text turns an active link color (which, by default, is red in HotJava), and the resource identified by the link is retrieved and displayed in HotJava.

In HotJava, images and applets are downloaded incrementally. This means that a page displayed in HotJava may have some of its images and applets displayed as gray boxes (to indicate they are in the process of being downloaded). This speeds up the chance for you to see something on other parts of the page while the page's images or applets download.

Movement

HotJava supports the functions **Back** and **Forward** as well as **Home**. Buttons along the bottom part of HotJava give you one-button access to these functions. (See the bottom of figure 9.1.) Access is also available through the **Navigate** option from the titlebar menu.

HotJava also allows you to open an arbitrary URL. You can use the titlebar selection **File / Open**, and then type the URL in the dialog box that appears. Alternately, you can enter the URL directly into the Document URL window at the top of the browser after deleting the URL that is currently displayed. This technique is very useful for opening a resource that is similar to the one already displayed; you can edit the text in the Document URL box and then press **Enter**.

Information Control

While information is being downloaded across the network, HotJava provides status messages on the bottom of the browser. Typically, this sequence of status message is:

```
Fetching...URL of the resource
Formatting...
[1 connection: xxxxx bytes remaining (xx% completed)]
Complete
```

This status sequence is very useful because it helps you determine where the possible problems in the browser operation might be. The status message shows the number of bytes remaining to be downloaded. By watching the progress of this number, you can make a guess about how long it will take to download the resource. If you judge this to be too long, HotJava provides the **Stop** button (stop sign icon at the bottom of figure 9.1). By clicking on **Stop**, you cancel the request and any downloading. A page that has had its text downloaded but images partially downloaded will still appear in the browser, with the special symbols described previously to indicate what images have not been downloaded.

The automatic downloading of images and applets can be turned off by selecting the **Options/ Properties** selection from the titlebar. The user can toggle on or off the Delay image loading and Delay applet loading options.

Interactivity

HotJava is designed to provide a high degree of interactivity through its display of applets, as described in Chapters 2 and 5.

HotJava also supports interactivity through person-to-person communication. HotJava recognizes `mailto` links that provide ways for you to bring up a session to send electronic mail. Figure 9.2 shows an electronic mail session that results from the user selecting a link at the bottom of the page shown in the HotJava browser. The link is:

```
<A Href="mailto:john@december.com">john@december.com</A>
```

Figure 9.2.
A HotJava mail session.

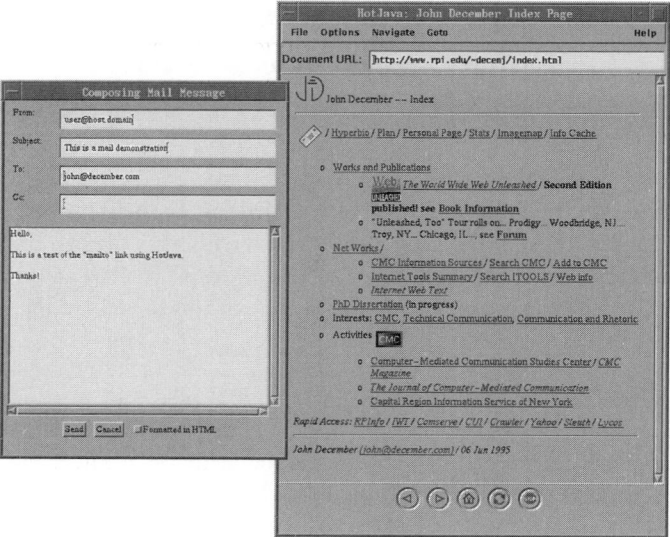

Security is an important part of the Java language (see Chapter 2) and the HotJava browser provides ways for the user to set policies and make choices about file access. Figure 9.3 shows the security dialog box brought up as a result of a selection of **Options** / **Security** from the titlebar menu.

Figure 9.3.
HotJava security options.

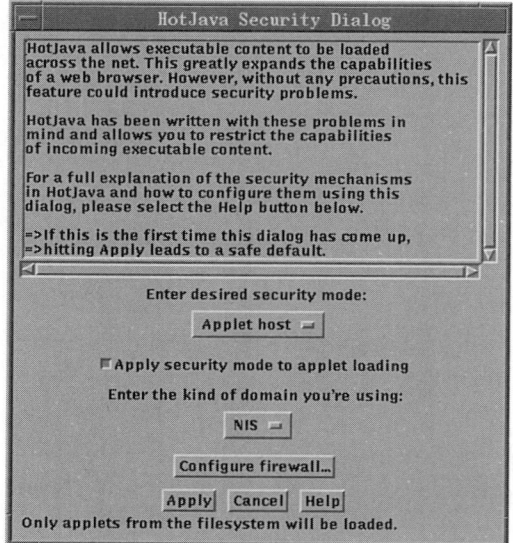

Using the security dialog box, you can toggle on or off the security modes for applet loading, as well as configure other security options such as identifying and configuring the firewall in place for your host or domain. This security dialog box, in addition to the security features of the Java language itself (see Chapter 2), acts as another line of defense where you can choose security options. For example, the dialog box allows you to load applets only from your own host or from within a firewall.

Options and Feedback

HotJava provides a large set of options for you to customize the browser. You can also get feedback about the browser's operation.

Feedback

The display of the current URL in the "Document URL" at the top of the browser is a very simple, yet extremely valuable, source of feedback. While navigating, this Document URL box shows what page is being downloaded or has been downloaded. This URL can also provide clues about the protocol of the information transfer, the originating host of the information, and filenames.

HotJava also gives feedback about the URLs of resources referred to in the hotspots on a page. By passing the mouse over any hotspot, the URL of the resource linked to that hotspot is displayed at the bottom of the browser. This gives you a chance to look before leaping into a resource.

As explained before with regard to information control, the status line at the bottom of the browser itself also gives you feedback about what the browser is doing and possible clues as to what is going on if the browser is not completing a retrieval.

Navigation Aids

The **Navigate** selection from the titlebar supports the following choices:

- **Forward.** Retrieves the next item in the history list of resources the browser has visited. This choice will be shaded if the browser is at the front of the history list.

- **Back.** Retrieves the previous item in the history list of resources the browser has visited. If you are at the temporal beginning of the history list, there is no resource "behind" the current one, so this option is shaded.

- **Home.** Retrieves the home or starting page for the browser.

- **Show History.** This pops up a window that shows a sequence of pages that you have visited during your current Java session. Note that this sequence is not necessarily the complete list of all visited pages. Because the Web branches with pages containing multiple links, recording your journey through the Web requires an algorithm to fill and flush a linear storage stack; this algorithm may nip off paths you have taken.

Figure 9.4 shows your path through a web of pages. Page A is connected via a hyperlink to page B, which is connected to page C. Page C is connected to both pages D and F. Page D is connected to page E.

Figure 9.4.

HotJava movement functions.

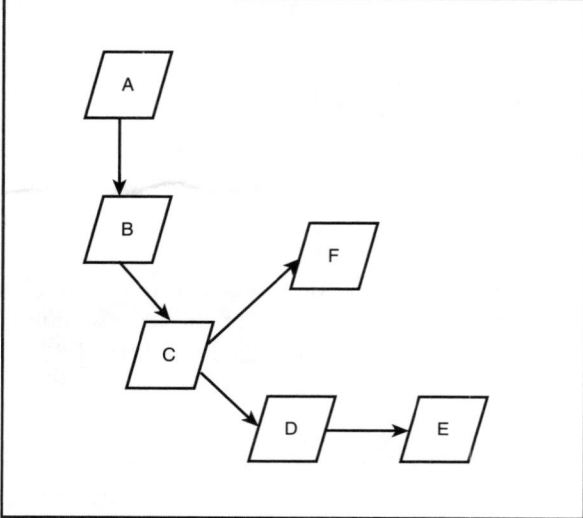

If you begin a HotJava session starting at page A and then follow the hyperlinks to page E, your history list would read:

- Page A
- Page B
- Page C
- Page D
- Page E

But if you then use the **Back** button twice to return to page C, and take the link from page C to page F, your history list would then read:

- Page A
- Page B
- Page C
- Page F

The page D and page E path would have been "nipped" from the history list because the browser could not store this non-linear tour of the pages in its linear stack. This is really no problem, as long as you realize that the history list is not a total history of all pages visited, but only the most recent linear path. Note also that this nipping would not occur if you had followed a link (if one existed) from page E to page F rather than using the **Back** button. (The **Back** button is what potentially causes this nipping to occur.) Also note that the history list is not maintained from session to session.

■ **Add Current to Hotlist.** This puts the resource currently displayed in HotJava on your hotlist. This hotlist is maintained from session to session in your personal disk area.

■ **Show Hotlist.** This option displays the current hotlist, allowing you to arbitrarily jump to any entry on it. Figure 9.5 shows an example hotlist.

Figure 9.5.
An example HotJava hotlist.

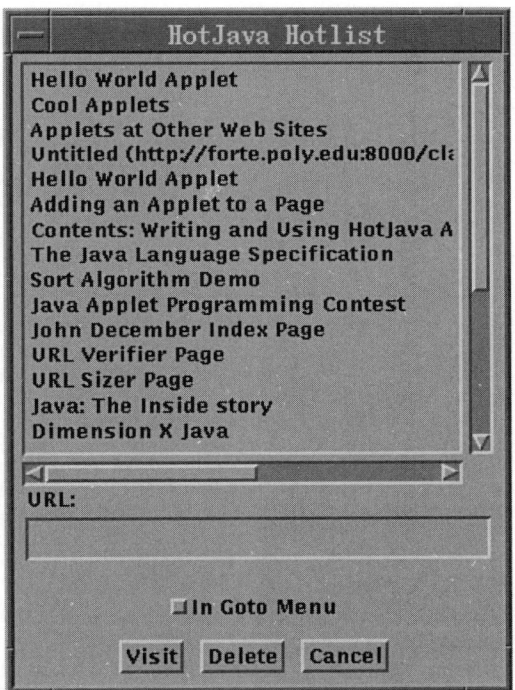

The hotlist is also connected to the **Goto** option on the titlebar. By selecting a URL in the hotlist, and then toggling on the "In Goto Menu" statement at the bottom of the hotlist dialog, the URL of that resource will be added to the Goto menu.

The **Goto** selection from the titlebar supports a "quick" form of the hotlist. You can add items to the **Goto** by selecting **Goto / Add Current**. This creates an entry for that item in the menu, creating a rapid access directory of resources. With the connection described previously, items from the hotlist can be quickly transferred to the **Goto** selection.

Built-In Information

HotJava supports a variety of online help information through the **Help** selection from the titlebar. This help includes:

■ Licensing information—registration, copyright, and license information.

■ Administrative information—browser version, bug reports, and the development team.

■ Documents—language specification, class libraries, man pages, users guide, and virtual machine specification.

■ Document search—query for keywords in the text of one or all of the documents (figure 9.6).

Figure 9.6.
Search HotJava
documentation.

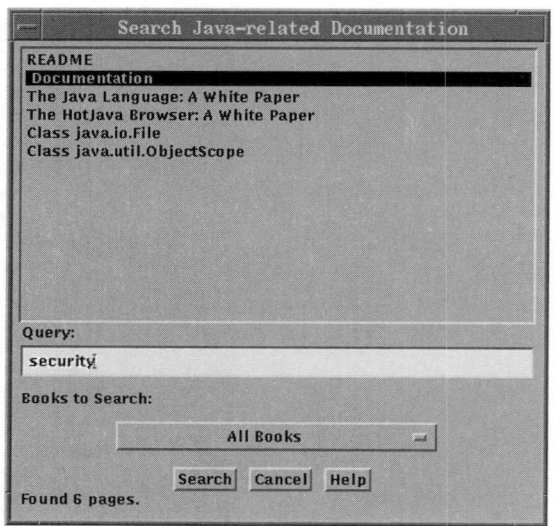

Options

HotJava supports a range of file management options through the **File** selection from the titlebar. These options include:

■ **Open.** This pops up a dialog box for you to enter the URL of a resource to retrieve.

■ **Reload.** This retrieves the resource identified by the current document URL. This is more than a refresh of the display; all the images and/or applets as well as text are retrieved across the network.

■ **Print.** Brings up a popup window allowing you to set printing options.

■ **View Source.** Brings up a popup window showing the HTML source of current resources.

■ **Quit.** Ends the current HotJava browser session.

The **Options** selection from the titlebar supports:

- **Security.** Options for setting security limitations and possible firewall configuration.
- **Properties.** You can set a variety of proxies. (See figure 9.7.) A proxy is a server that accepts URLs with a special prefix and returns the resource if found in a local cache.

Figure 9.7.
HotJava Browser
Options.

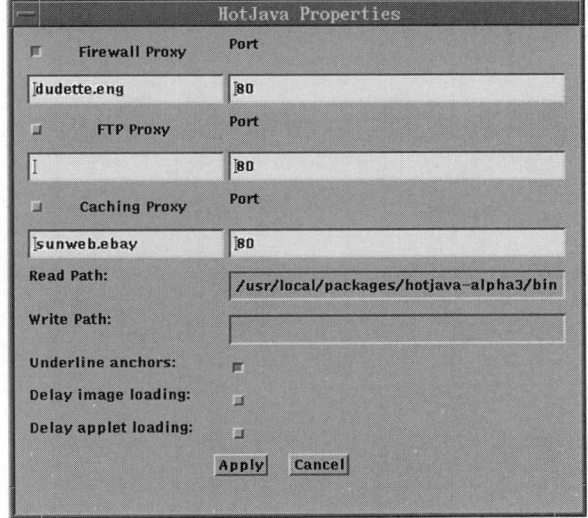

- **Flush Cache.** This removes the images that are stored in the browser's cache memory. If you revisit any page that contained these images, the browser will have to retrieve the image again.
- **Progress Monitor.** This brings up a popup window that shows the progress of downloading resources. Figure 9.8 shows the progress monitor as it is downloading a page. The monitor shows what resources need to be downloaded for a page (text, images, applets, and so on) and which ones have yet to be downloaded. This is additional and more detailed information than that provided by the status bar messages, particularly when multiple images and applets are being downloaded at once.

Figure 9.8.
HotJava progress monitor.

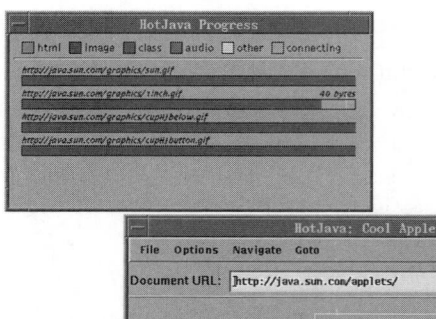

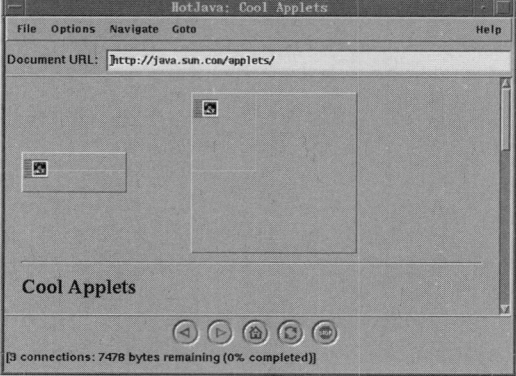

Web Actualization

The degree to which HotJava supports any user's feeling of having a "seamless" interface to Web information depends on your technical training, general Web navigation skills, and subjective experience. In general, you can increase your satisfaction with a Web browser by:

- Realizing what options are available;
- Knowing what needs these options meet; and
- Knowing how to use these options to accomplish useful work.

User Experience of the Web with HotJava

HotJava operates just like a non-Java Web browser by supporting your needs as a Web navigator. However, there are many special situations that may occur while using HotJava. These arise because of HotJava's capability to download executable content. This gives the content the capability to take control of the browser itself or launch special windows or other applications for user observation or interaction. These include animations, pop-ups, and an "autopilot mode," in which a Java applet takes control of the browser.

Animation

HotJava's ability to support executable content means that animation can be a part of what HotJava displays. Chapter 1 shows an example of Duke, Java's mascot, as he tumbles across the screen. Animations such as this will execute indefinitely because they are downloaded to your computer and run as a continuously looping program. Therefore, there is no way to stop an applet's animation if the applet itself doesn't provide an "off switch." It is good applet programming practice to provide such a switch.

Pop-Up Windows

Java applets may cause pop-up windows to appear and provide information or request information from the user. Some browser options cause windows to pop up for user interaction (for example the progress monitor in figure 9.8). Applets can also cause windows to pop up. For example, figure 9.9 shows the popup that occurs in the Surf-o-Matic demonstration applet.

Figure 9.9.
Autopilot pop-up window. (Courtesy of Patrick Chan, Sun Microsystems)

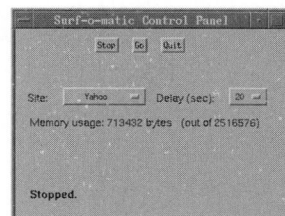
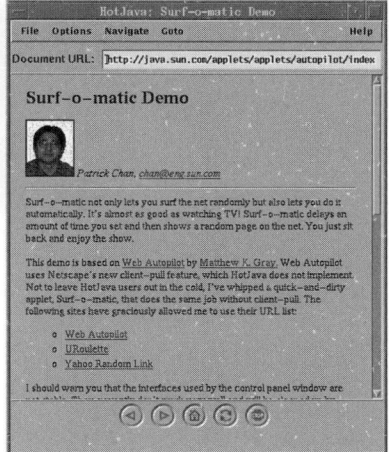

Browser Autopilot

The Surf-o-Matic demo shown in figure 9.9 also is an example of browser autopilot. By choosing the settings on the pop-up menu shown, you can choose to watch as the autopilot cruises through the Web.

Chapter Summary

This chapter described how the HotJava browser supports the needs of Web navigators. The HotJava interface gives you control over navigation functions as well as display options. HotJava can be used to display executable content as well as navigate the whole Web.

- HotJava supports information display, link activation, movement, information control, interactivity, options and feedback, and Web actualization.
- Using HotJava, you may experience animation, pop-up windows, or browser autopilot.

Developing Java Applications

The wonderful thing about Java is that it is not rocket science to use. It is a programming language, designed for similar intents and operating in ways similar to other programming languages that have preceded it. Java shares many characteristics with its immediate ancestor language, C++. Yet Java is stripped of some of the "powerful" features of C++ that can be maddening to people who have to maintain and upgrade source code.

The three chapters in this part survey the Java language, focusing on how you can write applications or applets in Java.

Alpha Java

These applets were made to compile under the alpha (1.3) release of Java. They may not work in later versions. Check this book's support web at `http://www.rpi.edu/~decemj/works/java.html` for any changes necessary to this code for it to compile under later versions of Java.

Chapter 10 reviews the features of Java that are procedural: data definition and control flow in programs. These features should be familiar conceptually and even syntactically to you if you have written programs in other computer languages such as C, C++, BASIC, Pascal, FORTRAN, or others.

However, Java is not a procedural language, but an object-oriented one. Chapter 11 explores Java's object-oriented features. Java supports the organization of software according to classes. Using hierarchies of classes, you can create reusable code and incrementally develop software.

Finally, Java uniquely combines computational and object-oriented features with the additional consideration of user-interface design. Chapter 12 surveys applet design and implementation by focusing on considerations for audience and purpose. How you craft an applet to fit the needs of the audience requires some consideration for design techniques. Applet implementation can follow a methodology that identifies classes, methods, and data.

The chapters in this part give you:

- An understanding of the framework for Java applications and applets, and how to compile, run, and use applets in Web pages
- Basic skills in defining data and program flow using Java language statements
- An appreciation for the object-oriented features of Java classes and subclasses
- Skills in creating classes and subclasses for Java applications and applets
- Insight into techniques for designing and implementing applets

---

Bug in Alpha HotJava

A bug in the alpha release of HotJava won't let the browser recognize changes you've made to applets if you restart HotJava in the classes subdirectory. Check to see the latest on this bug at the Sun Microsystems site at `http://java.sun.com/`.

Java Is a Programming Language

With Java, the Web is more than just an information delivery system; it is a system for interaction. This dramatic transformation of the Web relies on Java's features as a programming language. Java is not like the language for expressing the hypertext nature of the Web, Hypertext Markup Language (HTML), which is intended as a text markup language with only a fixed set of choices for expression. Instead, Java is an expressive programming language, allowing for much more manipulation of meaning and information. Java resembles the C++ language. Like C++, Java programmers can design flows of logic, manipulate data, and perform calculations. However, Java is dramatically different than C++ because Java supports the expression of interactive content for Web pages.

This chapter surveys Java from the perspective of how it supports procedural programming language features such as program structure, data definition, and control flow. Java also draws from the object-oriented paradigm for its organization and operation.

Programming Language Paradigms

■ **Procedural** languages view the world in terms of actions to process data in a linear flow. A procedural design might break up an action in a problem domain into smaller sub-actions. These sub-actions might then be implemented as procedures and functions that process information and data.

■ **Object-oriented** languages view the world in terms of objects that have a set of information (or data) and ways to operate on that information (methods) defined. An object-oriented design models parts of a problem domain in terms of objects. These objects maintain a current state in their data and behave according to how their methods manipulate that data or send messages to other objects.

The next chapter describes how Java is not just a procedural programming language like C, but one in which object-oriented concepts and features come into play. Chapter 12 introduces how you can design and implement Java applets to take advantage of all the features of Java: its procedural capabilities, its object-oriented nature, and its capability to create executable content.

The Essential Framework

Both conceptually and syntactically, a Java program is organized around classes. Programmers describe these classes using Java language statements and place these statements in files. These files are then compiled, and the resulting bytecodes are available for HotJava browsers to interpret.

An Essential Java Application

The "Hello, world" Java program shown in Chapter 2 is an example of a simple Java class that was an applet. An applet is a Java program that is intended to be compiled and interpreted by a Java-enabled browser. Another kind of Java program, called an application, is a standalone program that you can run independent of the HotJava browser. Remember that HotJava itself is a Java application.

Here is the source code for a very simple Java application. The source file is called `EssentialApplication.java`.

```
/**
  Program:      EssentialApplication
  Purpose:      simple demonstration of an Application
  @author       john@december.com
  @version      1.00; 17 July 1995
 */
```

```
class EssentialApplication {
   public static void main (String args[]) {
      System.out.println("Hello, world!");
   }
}
```

> **Note:** This Java source code example as well as others in this book were compiled using the alpha release of Java. For updates on these source code examples for beta and later releases of Java, see this book's support web at http://www.rpi.edu/~decemj/works/java.html.

Java's file organization follows a very common pattern. The source code file for EssentialApplication written in Java has the file extension .java. These statements define the flow of control and logic of the program when it executes. This file is then compiled using the Java compiler to produce a binary (machine readable) class file with the file extension .class.

A programmer could name a source code file any name, but the class file generated as a result of compilation is named *Class*.class by default. Therefore, a useful convention to keep track of the source code is to use the practices of:

- One class per file
- The file name is the same as the class name

You can compile EssentialApplication and run it from the command line (the operating system prompt is shown as a $ sign):

```
$ javac EssentialApplication.java
$ java EssentialApplication
Hello, world!
$
```

The first part of EssentialApplication.java is comments (from the opening /* to the closing */). These comments, ignored by the compiler, can be very useful to human readers of the source code. A good practice is to include administrative and other information in these comments. The comments shown use the @author and @version comment identifiers, which can be used in automatic document generating programs.

The real "meat" of this application is the declaration of the class EssentialApplication. The Java keyword class identifies that this is a class declaration. EssentialApplication is the name of the class and the opening curly brace { begins the class body. The body can contain data and operations called methods (procedural programming languages sometimes use the term "function" for these kinds of operations).

The EssentialApplication class contains just one method, the one method that *all* applications must have: main. The line

```
public static void main (String args[]) {
```

declares the function `main`. The words before the name of the function are keywords in Java that describe what kind of function `main` is. You'll understand the meaning of these words as you read about the details of the language in this and the next chapter. For now, remember that these keywords are a way of making the `main` method available for use by anyone else who would like to make an instance of the `EssentialApplication` class.

After the name of the method `main` is a list of the parameters for this method:

```
(String args[])
```

This parameter list consists of an array of objects of type `String`, a data type that is a class built into the Java language. The name of the array is parameter `args`. The `EssentialApplication` application does not use these parameters, but every `main` method *must* have this parameter list as a minimum. This parameter list holds the values of command line parameters that could be used with this application. For example, you can run the application with two parameters, but the output won't change:

```
$ java EssentialApplication alpha beta
Hello, world!
$
```

`EssentialApplication` reads the words `alpha` and `beta` from the command line and stores them in the array parameter with the name `args`.

Following the parameter list in the body of `EssentialApplication` is the body of the `main` method itself:

```
{
    System.out.println("Hello, world!");
}
```

This body is enclosed in the curly braces `{ }`. The single statement of the body accesses a method called `println`, which prints the string of characters `Hello, world!`.

This `EssentialApplication` doesn't do very much—its purpose is just to show you the minimal syntax necessary to write a Java application and to demonstrate how to compile and run it.

Making more elaborate applications than `EssentialApplication` requires that you gain more knowledge of Java's data representation, computational expressions, control flow, and class and object organization.

An Essential Java Applet

As you saw in Chapter 2 and Part II, an applet is the key to connecting Java content to Web pages displayed in a Java-enabled browser. An applet is a Java program that is meant to be referenced on a Web page using the HTML APP tag and interpreted by a Java-enabled browser. In contrast, as you saw with `EssentialApplication`, an application is a standalone program that can run without a browser. However, you write an applet using the Java language just as in applications. One difference between an application and an applet is that an applet lacks a `main` method. Here is a minimal applet:

```
import browser.Applet;
import awt.Graphics;
/**
 Program:     EssentialApplet
 Purpose:     simple demonstration of an Applet
 @author      john@december.com
 @version     1.00; 17 July 1995
 */
class EssentialApplet extends Applet {
   public void init() {
      resize(600, 300);
   }
   public void paint(Graphics context) {
      context.drawString("Hello, world!", 50, 100);
   }
}
```

This example is also stripped down to its essentials so that you can see how it works. In its structure, EssentialApplet still defines a class, just as EssentialApplication did. Also, like the application, this applet includes the features it "must" have to be a minimal applet.

The statements before the comments identify other Java source code that this minimal applet draws on for its functionality. These import statements make this other source code available to this applet:

```
import browser.Applet;
import awt.Graphics;
```

The names browser.Applet and awt.Graphics are part of Java's Application Programming Interface (API). The API contains packages of classes that you can use in writing Java applets and applications. You can find complete documentation of the API through the Help selection if you are using a HotJava browser, or from Sun's Java site at http://java.sun.com/.

The declaration of this applet:

```
class EssentialApplet extends Applet
```

identifies EssentialApplet as a subclass of the Applet class. This gives objects, which are declared as type EssentialApplet, many built-in features that are inherited from the Applet class's functionality.

The body of the applet contains two methods that an applet must have: init, to initialize the size of the applet for display purposes on the Web page, and paint to actually do the rendering of the visual representation of this applet.

The paint method includes a required parameter of type Graphics called in this applet context. The context object is used in the body of the paint method to actually do the "work" of this applet—drawing the string "Hello, world!" at a location given by the coordinates 50 and 100:

```
      context.drawString("Hello, world!", 50, 100);
```

The programmer can place the source code for this applet in a file named EssentialApplet.java and then compile it:

```
$ javac EssentialApplet.java
```

However, you cannot run an applet directly from the command line; if you try this, the Java interpreter will complain:

```
$ java EssentialApplet
In class EssentialApplet: void main(String argv[]) is not defined
$
```

The Java interpreter was looking for a main function in the code, believing that you wanted to run a Java application from the command line.

Instead, you need to create an HTML file, perhaps calling it EssentialApplet.html.

```
<HTML>
<!-- Purpose: HTML file to hold reference to applet. -->
<!-- Author: john@december.com -->
<!-- Version: 1.10; 21 July 1995 -->
<HEAD>
    <TITLE>Essential Applet Web Interface</TITLE>
</HEAD>
<BODY>
    <P>Essential to an applet: <APP Class="EssentialApplet">
</BODY>
</HTML>
```

The file that you've created by compiling EssentialApplet.java is EssentialApplet.class. The directory structure of Java is organized so that by default it looks for class files referenced in an APP tag in a directory called classes. The classes directory should be in the same directory as the EssentialApplet.html source file. When the user opens the file EssentialApplet.html in a Java-enabled browser, the applet paints the string "Hello, world!" in the browser window. (Refer to figure 2.3.)

Now that you've seen the essentials of both a Java application and an applet, the next step is to gain some more knowledge of Java structure and syntax.

Java Program Features

The examples of an application and an applet showed you the conceptual essentials of programming in Java. The rest is more elaborate, involving more language constructs, more ways to share code among classes, and file management and network resource retrieval techniques.

Java has many syntax features that set the stage for programming:

■ Java *is* case-sensitive. The class name EssentialApplet is different from Essentialapplet. By convention, class names are capitalized, and method and object names start with small letters.

■ Comments in Java can be in several styles:
```
/* comments can be on
   several lines using the forward slash and star to start and
   the star and forward slash to end
*/
```

```
// two forward slashes identify a comment for the rest of the line.

/** The forward slash and double star is a proposed way to
    identify comments that can be used in automatic
    documentation generation. These comments can go over
    several lines and may contain special
    comment keywords such as @author and @version.
*/
```

-- Java ignores "whitespace" and comments. A Java program's layout on the page is for human convenience only. As far as the Java compiler is concerned, here is an equivalent version of the EssentialApplication example:

```
class EssentialApplication{public static void main
(String args[]){System.out.println("Hello, world!");}}
```

■ Layout conventions for Java programs often follow those developed out of C and C++ programming practices. Java programmers often indent their statements to reflect their hierarchy and line up the ending curly braces { to reflect the nesting of the program statements.

■ Java uses ; as a statement separator and { } as a statement grouper.

Java Procedural Features

Java has features to represent data, describe computation, and control the flow of a program's logic. If you are familiar with C++ or C, you'll see that Java resembles these languages in its syntax and data flow.

Essential Java Data

The "Essential" demonstration programs of a Java application and applet were stripped down so much that they didn't demonstrate how a Java program can be used to represent data. Here is a Java application that demonstrates data representation, using the data types that a programmer of another computer language would probably recognize:

```
/**
 Program:    EssentialData
 Purpose:    simple demonstration of Java data representation.
 @author     john@december.com
 @version    1.00; 21 July 1995
 */

class EssentialData {

  public static void main (String args[]) {

    int     myInteger   = 42;
    float   myReal      = 3.14159;
    String  someName    = "Mr. Kyle";
    boolean myTruth     = true;
    int     myArray[]   = {1856, 1984};
```

```
        System.out.println(myInteger);
        System.out.println(myReal);
        System.out.println(someName);
        System.out.println(myTruth);
        System.out.println(myArray[0]);
        System.out.println(myArray[1]);
        System.out.println(args[0]);
        System.out.println(args[1]);
        System.out.println(args[2]);
    }
}
```

If you compile and run this application with three parameters on its command line, you get:

```
$ javac EssentialData.java
$ java EssentialData alpha beta gamma
42
3.14159
Mr. Kyle
true
1856
1984
alpha
beta
gamma
$
```

This `EssentialData` application demonstrates the essential data types built into the Java language. The statement:

```
int     myInteger   = 42;
```

defines a variable named `myInteger`, which is type `int`. At the same time, this statement also initializes this variable's value to 42. Similarly, the next lines of the application define a real number (`float`), a variable representing strings of characters, and a Boolean variable, `myTruth`, which can take on exactly one of the values of `true` or `false`.

After the declarations and initializations of these variables, the application prints them using statements using one of Java's output methods, `println`:

```
System.out.println(myInteger);
```

You can declare a variable to be an array. The variable `myArray` with the `[]` symbol after its name indicates it is an array.

```
int
myArray[] = {1856, 1984};;
```

The variable `myArray` is an array of integers (of type `int`). This array is also initialized to two values shown in curly braces: `{1856, 1984}`. To reference these values, you can write the array name with the element's index in square brackets after it. The array is indexed beginning with element `0`. So a reference to `myArray[0]` is to the first element of the array, which is initialized to `1856`.

Why Start Counting with 0?

The design of the Java language was heavily influenced by the programming languages C++ and C. In C++ and C, array indexes start with 0. C programmers can get very adamant about this feature, and it sometimes can affect their thinking in strange ways. Some C programmers can think of chapters numbered 0, houses numbered starting with 0, or might refer to their first child as "child 0."

The array myArray isn't the only array in EssentialData. The command line parameters were also stored in an array declared in the parameter list for the application's main method: (String args[]). This array was not given values until the program was run. At runtime, the parameters were stored in an array of strings called args. You can reference these parameters just as you would any other string in Java. For example, here is an application that references its parameters by printing them out:

```
/**
 Program:     EssentialParams Class
 Purpose:     demonstrate writing out parameters;
 @author      john@december.com
 @version     1.01; 22 July 1995
 */

class EssentialParams{
    public static void main (String args[]) {
        int counter;
        for (counter = 0; counter < args.length; counter++)
            System.out.println(args[counter]);
      }
}
```

You can compile and run this example application. When you run it, it will echo the parameters you send to it:

```
$ javac EssentialParamss.java
$ java EssentialParamss regular cafe almond
regular
cafe
almond
```

Notice that the method length can be used on an array name to get the length of the array. In the for loop in the main method, the counter goes from 0 (which holds the array element for the first parameter) to 2 (one less than the length of the array of parameters).

Arrays can also be two-dimensional:

```
/**
 Program:     EssentialArrays Class
 Purpose:     demonstrate Java array of arrays;
 @author      john@december.com
 @version     1.00; 22 July 1995
 */
```

```
class EssentialArrays{
   public static void main (String args[]) {

      int myTable[][] = new int [2][3];  // this statement sets up a two-
      dimensional array

      System.out.println("This is an array of arrays...");

      myTable[0][0] = 1;
      myTable[0][1] = 2;
      myTable[0][2] = 3;
      myTable[1][0] = 4;
      myTable[1][1] = 5;
      myTable[1][2] = 6;

      System.out.print(myTable[0][0]);
      System.out.print(myTable[0][1]);
      System.out.println(myTable[0][2]);

      System.out.print(myTable[1][0]);
      System.out.print(myTable[1][1]);
      System.out.println(myTable[1][2]);
   }
}
```

This example produces the output:

```
This is an array of arrays...
123
456
```

There are more simple data types in Java, which you can use for more precise calculations. See Appendix B for a list of these data types.

More Details on Names and Literals

In Java, like in any programming language, you have to name many things. You'll have to name classes, variables, and methods. The names for any of these identifiers follow these rules:

- A name cannot be a Java reserved keyword that is used for the "scaffolding" of a Java program. (See Appendix B for a list of these reserved keywords.)
- A name must start with a letter (upper- or lowercase), or an underscore _ or dollar sign $.
- After the first character, a name can have any other character (such as numbers) except special reserved characters used in the language. (See Appendix B for a table of these reserved characters.)

In other words, you can be pretty expressive in naming things in Java, keeping within its naming rules. In actual practice, you should develop a consistent, coherent naming scheme that helps readers of your programs understand your program. The naming scheme is totally up to a you, but some conventions include:

- Nouns as names for classes. For example: Car, Bus, Trolley.
- Verbs as names for methods. For example: start, slowdown, stop.

- Initial capital letters for class names.
- All lowercase letters for method names.
- Uppercase letters to distinguish among words. For example: SubwayCar, IgnitionSwitch, fixEngine.

The above conventions arise out of object-oriented programming culture. In actual practice, Java programmers can come up with whatever conventions are suitable to their application. The fundamental goal, however, should be *meaningful* names. Older languages such as early FORTRAN only allowed a certain number of characters for names; there is no restriction in Java (except for some memory storage system limits).

Good naming actually plays a large role in the readability of a program. And given that computer programs are read and maintained much more often than they are written, meaningful names may be an important contributor to overall software quality. Consider the following Java method:

```
public void TUP(T t3){t3.stg++;}
```

What does it do? This could be maddening to a programmer looking through a program to find out what is happening. In contrast,

```
public void raiseTemperature(Temperature currentTemperature)
    {currentTemperature.setting++;}
```

is more understandable. The `raiseTemperature` method requires more characters to type, but while a programmer may type but once, readers of the code may have to decipher it dozens of times. Good naming practices can help those poor souls who maintain software and must continually untangle the "power" of terse but obtuse code.

Essential Java Literals

Literals are values that variables can have. For example, an example integer literal is 1856. The following application demonstrates how literals can be expressed and displayed in a variety of ways:

```
/**
Program:    EssentialLiterals
Purpose:    simple demonstration of Java data literals.
@author     john@december.com
@version    1.00; 21 July 1995
*/

class EssentialLiterals {

  public static void main (String args[]) {

      System.out.println("INTEGER (BASE 10)");
      System.out.println(10);         // This is a base 10 integer
      System.out.println(4294967295); // large 32 bit integer (int)
      System.out.println(9223372036854775807L);
                                      // large 64 bit integer (L on end = long)
      System.out.println(2E3);        // scientific notation: 2 times 1,000
```

```
        System.out.println("INTEGERS IN OTHER BASES");
        System.out.println(010);       // A leading 0 means octal (base 8)
        System.out.println(0x10);      // A leading 0x means hexidicemal (base 16)

        System.out.println("BASE 16");
        System.out.println(0xA);       // A in base 16 is the digit for 10
        System.out.println(0xB);       // B in base 16 is the digit for 11
        System.out.println(0xC);       // C in base 16 is the digit for 12
        System.out.println(0xD);       // D in base 16 is the digit for 13
        System.out.println(0xE);       // E in base 16 is the digit for 14
        System.out.println(0xF);       // F in base 16 is the digit for 15

        System.out.println("BOOLEAN");
        System.out.println(true);
        System.out.println(false);

        System.out.println("FLOATING POINT");
        System.out.println(3.1415);         // real number
        System.out.println(-0.61803);       // negative real number
        System.out.println(2.9E4);          // scientific notation: 2.9 times 10,000

        System.out.println("STRINGS");
        System.out.println("");                   // empty string
        System.out.println("\"Hi, Lorrie.\""); // quote in string
        System.out.println("one\ntwo");           // linebreak in string
        System.out.println("hot\tjava");          // tab in string
    }
}
$ javac EssentialLiterals.java
$ java EssentialLiterals
INTEGER (BASE 10)
10
4294967295
9223372036854775807
2000
INTEGERS IN OTHER BASES
8
16
BASE 16
10
11
12
13
14
15
BOOLEAN
true
false
FLOATING POINT
3.1415
-0.61803
29000
STRINGS

"Hi, Lorrie."
one
two
hot     java
```

Essential Java Operators

Java has all the necessary operators to perform calculations with variables declared with its built-in data types. This class demonstrates how you perform the familiar operations in Java:

```java
/**
Program:    EssentialOperators
Purpose:    simple demonstration of Java operators.
@author     john@december.com
@version    1.02; 21 July 1995
*/

class EssentialOperators {
   public static void main (String args[]) {

      int     myInteger   = 42;
      float   myReal      = 3.14159;
      String  someName    = "Mr. Kyle";
      boolean myTruth     = true;
      int     myArray[]   = {1856, 1984};

      System.out.println("UNARY OPERATORS");
      System.out.println(-myInteger);  // negate an integer
      System.out.println(-myReal);     // negate a real number
      System.out.println(myInteger++); // display the number then add 1 to it
      System.out.println(myInteger--); // display the number then subtract 1

      System.out.println("BINARY OPERATORS");
      System.out.println(myInteger + 100);    // addition
      System.out.println(myInteger - myReal); // subtraction
      System.out.println(100 * myReal);       // multiplication
      System.out.println(myInteger/3.0);      // division with real
      System.out.println(myInteger/3);        // division without remainder
      System.out.println(myReal/3);           // real division

      System.out.println(myInteger%3);        // modulo arithmetic shows
                                              // remainder after dividing by 3

      System.out.println("RELATIONAL OPERATORS");
      System.out.println(myInteger  32);      // greater than
      System.out.println(myInteger >= 32);    // greater than or equal to
      System.out.println(myInteger
```

```
$ javac EssentialOperators.java
$ java EssentialOperators
UNARY OPERATORS
-42
-3.14159
42
43
BINARY OPERATORS
142
38.8584
314.159
14
14
1.0472
0
RELATIONAL OPERATORS
```

```
false
false
true
true
true
false
BOOLEAN OPERATORS
false
false
true
true
false
true
false
Mr. Kyle is cool.
Mr. Kyle, the answer is 42
```

To master the full details of working with operators in Java, there are two key issues to understand: precedence and typecasting.

Precedence is the order in which operators are evaluated. Precedence for a programming language is set by rules stating which operators get evaluated first. Without these rules, statements such as:

```
3 + 4 * 2
```

could be ambiguous: Is the answer 14 (seven times two) or 11 (three plus eight)? The rules of mathematics say that the answer is 11; a Java compiler would also agree and call this 11, because Java places higher precedence on the multiplication operator (*) than addition. The 4 * 2 part of the expression gets evaluated first (even though this expression doesn't read that way from left to right). Grouping symbols with parentheses can force a different precedence:

```
(3 + 4) * 2
```

This expression is evaluated by starting inside the parentheses first: 3 plus 4 is 7; 7 times 2 is 14. Java's rules for operator precedence are defined by the following categories, going from the highest precedence to the lowest. Operators in the same precedence category are evaluated from left to right. Some of these operators have not yet been discussed here, but are defined in Appendix B of this book.

1. `.  []  ()`
   The `.` operator is used for resolving names. For example, the previous examples used the method `System.out.println`. The periods in the name actually are operators that help the compiler determine which method is being referenced.

2. `++ -- ! ~ instanceof`

3. `* / %`

4. `+ -`

5. `> >>>`

6. `=`

7. == !=

8. &

9. ^

10. ¦

11. &&

12. ¦¦

13. ?:

14. = op=

15. ,

The next important term in working with variables and expressions is *casting*. Casting means that you change an expression from one data type to another. For example, a real expression can be cast as an integer with its fraction part truncated, or an integer, Boolean, or floating expression can be cast as a string. Here is a class that demonstrates casting:

```java
/**
Program:     EssentialCasting
Purpose:     simple demonstration of Java operators and casting.
@author      john@december.com
@version     1.02; 21 July 1995
*/

class EssentialCasting {

    public static void main (String args[]) {

        int     myInteger  = 42;
        float   myReal     = 3.987;
        boolean myTruth    = true;
        String  aPhrase;
        float   aReal;
        float   anInteger;

        anInteger = (int)myReal;                // floating to integer
        System.out.println(anInteger);

        aReal = myInteger + 0.001;              // floating expression
        System.out.println(aReal);

        aPhrase = "Survey says: " + myInteger; // integer to string
        System.out.println(aPhrase);

        aPhrase = "Survey says: " + myTruth;   // boolean to string
        System.out.println(aPhrase);

    }
}
```

Running this example yields:

```
$ java EssentialCasting
3
```

```
42.001
Survey says: 42
Survey says: true
```

This class demonstrates how casting can be explicit, using the casting operator. For example, you can cast a real number to an integer like this:

```
anInteger = (int)myReal;
```

Casting can also be implicit. For example, when you write an expression that will be assigned to a string variable, the variables in the expression can be changed to the strings. For example, the statement in EssentialCasting:

```
aPhrase = "Survey says: " + myInteger;
```

uses implicit casting to convert the value of myInteger to a string so that it can be appended to the string Survey says.

Essential Expressions

Java also supports many mathematical expressions and special functions through the Java Math class:

```
/**
 Program:     EssentialExpress Class
 Purpose:     demonstrate Java math expressions;
 @author      john@december.com
 @version     1.02; 22 July 1995
 */

class EssentialExpress{
   public static void main (String args[]) {

      double example;    // double precision is available for math

      //math operations are available:
      example = (3+2) + 5*3/7 + 3.123 + (42*7 + 4);
      System.out.println("example result = " + example);

      //common math functions are available:
      example = Math.sin(0.50) + Math.log(13) + Math.sqrt(2) + Math.exp(4);
      System.out.println("example result = " + example);

      //other functions:
      System.out.println("absolute value of -3 = " + Math.abs(-3));
      System.out.println("a random number (0.0 to 1.0) = " + Math.random());
      System.out.println("round(3.65) = " + Math.round(3.65));
      System.out.println("2 to the third power (2*2*2) = " + Math.pow(2, 3));
      System.out.println("maximum of 3.98 and 14.2 = " + Math.max(3.98, 14.2));
   }
}
```

Here is the output:

```
$ javac EssentialExpress.java
$ java EssentialExpress
example result = 308.123
```

```
example result = 59.0567
absolute value of -3 = 3
a random number (0.0 to 1.0) = 0.396465
round(3.65) = 4
2 to the third power (2*2*2) = 8
maximum of 3.98 and 14.2 = 14.2
```

Essential Flow

All the preceding constructs are essential to building the scaffolding and the "guts" of a Java program. However, if you want to make a Java program actually do something more complicated, you'll have to learn to create more than a single top-to-bottom pass over a series of assignment and computation statements. Program control flow is a key part of any programming language, and Java has everything you need to express any logical flow of control.

Flow control involves:

- **Branching.** Sending the flow of control in a program to a statement or block of statements based on whether a given condition is true or not. (See figure 10.1.)
- **Looping.** Sending the flow of control in the program several times (or none) on a block of statements. (See figure 10.2.)

Figure 10.1.
Branching program control.

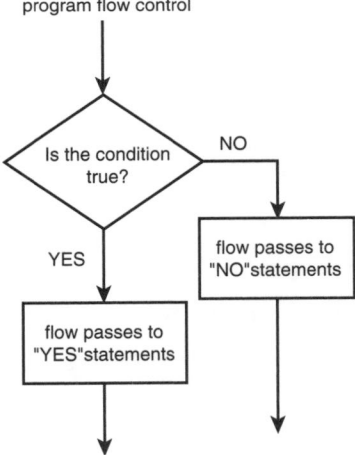

The reason you would use branching is to make decisions in programming. You would use looping to repeat an operation until some condition is fulfilled. Java supports several constructs to achieve both branching and looping.

Figure 10.2.
*Looping program
control.*

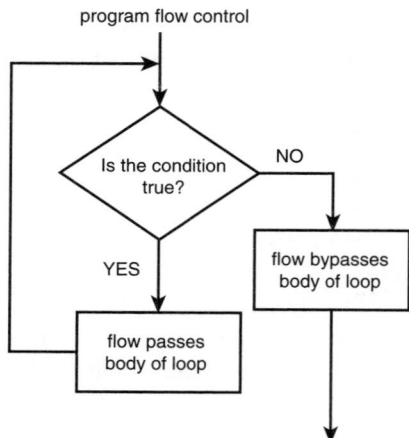

This application demonstrates the essential features for program flow in Java:

```
/**
 Program:    EssentialFlow
 Purpose:    simple demonstration of Java control flow
 @author     john@december.com
 @version    1.03; 21 July 1995
 */

class EssentialFlow{
   public static void main (String args[]) {

      System.out.println("BRANCHING");
      // If-then branching.

      boolean OK = true;

      // This is a simple if-then statement.
      if (OK)
         System.out.println("OK.");
      else
         System.out.println("NOT OK.");

      // Quick version of if-then branching.

      OK ? System.out.println("Quick OK.") :
         System.out.println("Quick NOT OK.");

      // Mutiple line if-then branches.

      if (OK) {
         System.out.println("This is");
         System.out.println("remaining OK.");
         }
      else {
         System.out.println("Or is it");
         System.out.println("NOT OK?");
         }
```

```java
// SWITCH type branching

int temperature = 37;
switch (temperature){
   case (0):
      System.out.println("Freezing water!");
      break;
   case (37):
      System.out.println("Human body.");
      break;
   case (100):
      System.out.println("Boiling water!");
      break;
   default:
      System.out.println("Some temperature.");
}

System.out.println("LOOPING");

// Simple FOR loop up.
int counter;

for (counter = 1; counter  0; counter--){
   System.out.println("Hi down: " + counter);
   };

// FOR loop with non-unit step sizes.
for (counter = -50;
     counter < 99;
     counter = counter + 50){
     System.out.println("Hi again: " + counter");
     }
  // WHILE loop with condition checked at the start.
  counter  = 0;
  OK  = true;
  while (OK) {
      System.out.println("Still OK: " + counter);
      counter++;
      OK = (counter < 3);
      }
   // DO-WHILE loop executes at least once; condition check at end.
   counter  = 500;
   OK  = true;
   do {
       System.out.println("OK = " + OK + " counter = " + counter);
       counter++;
       OK = (counter < 3);
     } while (OK);
   }
}
```

```
$ javac EssentialFlow.java
$ java EssentialFlow
BRANCHING
OK.
Quick OK.
This is
remaining OK.
```

```
Human body.
LOOPING
Hi up: 1
Hi up: 2
Hi down: 3
Hi down: 2
Hi down: 1
Hi again: -50
Hi again: 0
Hi again: 50
Still OK: 0
Still OK: 1
Still OK: 2
OK = true counter = 500
```

The Java language supports labeled branching and more complicated break statements. However, good programming practice generally eschews arbitrary branching to labels in a program because breaks and goto statements can be hard to follow. Well-designed flow statements without labeled branching can achieve any logical flow of control in a program.

Essential Methods

Creating variables and defining the flow of control are the basics for programming in a computer language. With these statements, theoretically, a programmer could create any computer program. However, a long program would get quickly complicated, turning into one, huge, monstrous file of code.

A programmer's goal should be to aim for creating manageable size code units to assist in both writing and reading a program. Creating chunks of code that can be reused is a key technique for developing manageable software programs. In Java, a method fulfills this role. Here is an example method:

```java
public static void repeater (String line, int times) {
    int counter;
    for (counter = 1; counter <= times; counter ++) {
        System.out.println(line);
    }
}
```

This method is called repeater and it is, like the main method used in the previous examples, available for use by anyone (public), associated with the class in which it is defined (static) and returns no value after it executes (void). Unlike main, however, this method's name is programmer defined; there is no predefined method by this name. The body of repeater declares a variable counter and uses it in a for loop to print out a string a given number of times. This method is not really all that useful in itself, but is a "little tool" that—when used with other methods—can be a part of a more powerful program. Here is an example application that demonstrates the repeater function used in a class:

```
/**
 Program:    EssentialMethods
 Purpose:    simple demonstration of java methods
 @author     john@december.com
 @version    1.02; 22 July 1995
 */

class EssentialMethods {

    public static void main (String args[]) {
        greeter("Hello, methods.");
        greeter(waver(3));
    }

    public static void greeter (String greeting) {
        repeater(greeting, 1);
    }

    public static String waver (int waves) {
        repeater("WAVE", waves);
        return("Done waving.");
    }

    public static void repeater (String line, int times) {
        int counter;
        for (counter = 1; counter <= times; counter ++) {
            System.out.println(line);
        }
    }
}
```

This application merely prints out several strings in response to the flow of control defined by the function calls in the main method. The main method of an application is its "engine" that gets called first and starts off the flow of control in a program. In the body of main, the method greeter is called, first with a string, Hello, methods, and then with a method call, waver(3). The method waver is declared as public static String, meaning that it will return a String value as a result of its execution. The body of waver shows that this return value is a string stating Done waving. This string is then used as the parameter in greeter.

Note that a method can be referenced in a class before it is declared and defined in that class. Both greeter and waver call repeater to do the printing. This is a subtle point, but could be very valuable for later code maintenance: all printing is encapsulated in one method.

If you decide to later alter the way printing should be done, you only have to change the body of repeater, and just one print statement.

Figure 10.3 shows the calling sequence and parameter passing that happens when this application executes:

Figure 10.3.
*Method calling pattern
in* EssentialMethods.

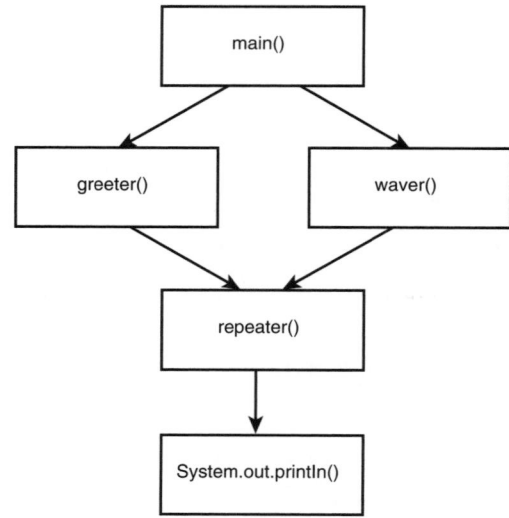

This is the output:

```
$ javac EssentialMethods.java
$ java EssentialMethods
Hello, methods.
WAVE
WAVE
WAVE
Done waving.
```

Scoping Rules

Creating methods in a Java program allows you to define variables inside method bodies. For example, the variable counter inside repeater is declared as type int and used in the for loop. This variable is local to the repeater method and is not a valid reference outside of its body; the *scope* of counter is said to be the method repeater. Scope is the location in a program code where a variable is available for reference.

Here is an example application that demonstrates scope and constants in Java:

```
/**
   Program:    EssentialScope
   Purpose:    simple demonstration of Java scope and constants
   @author     john@december.com
   @version    1.03; 22 July 1995
*/

class EssentialScope {

    static int counter = 10;
    static final int MAXIMUM = 99;

    public static void main (String args[]) {
```

```
        // Illegal: MAXIMUM = 900; Can't assign values to final variables

        System.out.println("main: counter = " + counter);
        System.out.println("main: MAXIMUM = " + MAXIMUM);
        alpha();
        beta();
        gamma(counter);
        System.out.println("main: counter = " + counter);
    }

    public static void alpha() {
        System.out.println("alpha: counter = " + counter);
        System.out.println("alpha: MAXIMUM = " + MAXIMUM);
    }

    public static void beta() {
        int counter = 900;
        System.out.println("beta: counter = " + counter);
        System.out.println("beta: EssentialScope.counter = " + EssentialScope.counter);
    }

    public static void gamma(int counter) {
        int gammaCounter = 500; // undefined variable outside of gamma

        counter = counter + 100;
        System.out.println("gamma: counter = " + counter);
        System.out.println("gamma: gammaCounter = " + gammaCounter);
    }
}
```

This class defines two variables, counter and MAXIMUM. These are defined as static, which means they are associated with the class EssentialScope rather than with instances of the class. (The difference between a class and instances will be explained in detail in the next chapter on Java's object-oriented qualities.) The identifier MAXIMUM has the keyword final in its declaration, making it a constant (the word static does *not* make an identifier a constant). By convention, constants are often written using all capital letters.

Here is the application's output:

```
$ javac EssentialScope.java
$ java EssentialScope
main: counter = 10
main: MAXIMUM = 99
alpha: counter = 10
alpha: MAXIMUM = 99
beta: counter = 900
beta: EssentialScope.counter = 10
gamma: counter = 110
gamma: gammaCounter = 500
main: counter = 10
```

Within the bodies of the other methods in this class, counter and MAXIMUM are available for reference. However, MAXIMUM cannot be assigned a new value. The print statements in the class demonstrate references to these variables:

- The alpha method shows how the scope of the class identifiers extend into the method bodies.

- The beta method shows how an identifier with the same name as a class identifier "hides" the class identifier. The first print statement in beta shows the local counter. The second print statement shows how the class identifier scope can be accessed by referring to the class name, followed by a period and then the identifier: EssentialScope.counter. So while the class identifier is "hidden" behind the local identifier with the same name, the class identifier is available for reference through its class name.

- The gamma method has a declaration for an identifier, gammaCounter, whose scope is limited to that method only. The identifier counter is in gamma's parameter list; this value can be changed inside the body of gamma, but such changes are limited only to the body of gamma. The class identifier counter remains unaltered by the changes to gamma's counter.

Java Runnable Features

The examples of applications shown here are the basics of Java's procedural features. However, Java can do much more. You can use it to create an "animated" page.

To allow Java programmers to create applications that execute code, the Java language provides an interface called Runnable. An interface is a collection of methods that can be used by a Java class. The Runnable interface gives a Java programmer a set of functionality to create "active" applets. When you create a class that implements the Runnable interface, you must define all the methods in that interface. Here is the definition of an application that does this:

```
import awt.*;
import browser.Applet;
/**
 Program:     EssentialRunner application
 Purpose:     simple demonstration of a runnable applet
 @author      john@december.com
 @version     1.54; 22 July 1995
 */
public class EssentialRunner extends Applet implements Runnable {

    private Thread flow;
    boolean done, pause;
    static int width = 500;
    static int height = 500;

    static int interval = 5;
    int x, y, cycle;

    public void init() {
        resize(width, height);
```

```
    }

    public void paint(Graphics g) {     // this method draws the applet
        g.SetColor(Color.green);
        g.drawLine(width/2, width/2, x, y);
        y = y + interval;
        if (y > width) {
            y = 0;
            cycle++;
            if ((cycle%2) == 0)
                x = cycle*interval;
            else
                x = width - cycle*interval;
        }
    }

    public void update(Graphics g) {
        paint(g);
    }

    public void start() {
        done = false;
        pause = false;
        x = 0;
        y = 0;
        cycle = 0;
        flow = new Thread(this);
        flow.start();
    }

    public void run() {
        try {
            while (!done) {
        Thread.sleep(interval);
                if (!pause) repaint();
            }
        }
    }

    public void stop() {
        done = true;
        flow.stop();
    }

    public void mouseUp(int x, int y) {
        pause = !pause;
    }
}
```

Figure 10.4 shows a still image of the output of the EssentialRunner applet.

Figure 10.4.
EssentialRunner
output.

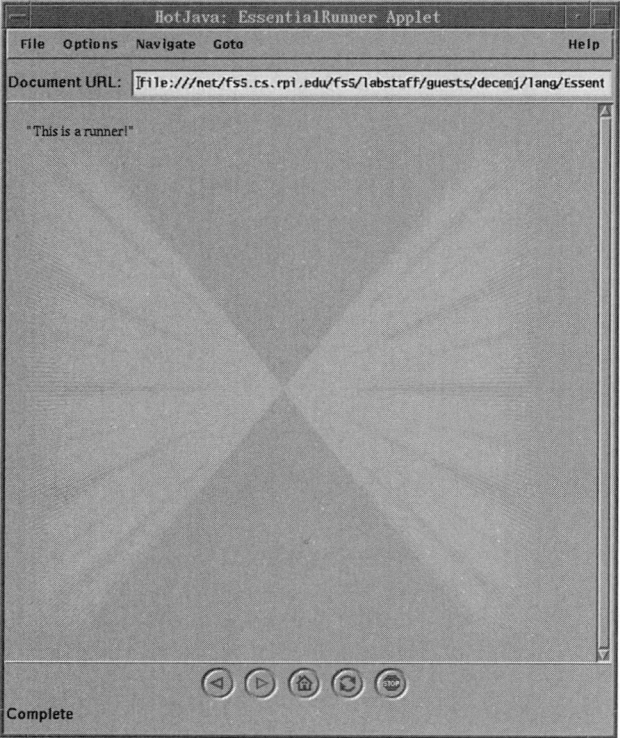

The applet continually paints lines on the screen. If you place the cursor on the browser window where the applet is displayed, you can click and release the mouse to stop the painting. The applet will start again with another mouse click and release. This application shows the basics of a Runnable applet: the run method is started first and serves as the "engine" of the applet. The start method is the first one called. A key line is:

```
flow = new Thread(this);
```

This line creates an object that is type Thread, which is associated with the EssentialRunner class. The EssentialRunner class passes a pointer of itself to create a new Thread object by the this keyword. The flow thread serves as a way to control the pace of the activity in the applet. For example, in the run method, this line:

```
Thread.sleep(interval);
```

pauses the action for a short time (interval is set at five milliseconds). The most complicated method of EssentialRunner is its paint method, which calculates the coordinates for a new line to draw using the previous coordinates and a cycle variable.

Online Java Programmer's Reference

Sun Microsystem's Java site `http://java.sun.com/` is a great source for documentation on Java. In particular:

■ *The Java Programmer's Guide* (`http://java.sun.com/progGuide/java/TOC.html`) gives many online step-by-step lessons about Java.

■ Java Documentation (`http://java.sun.com/documentation.html`) gives many links to Java documentation online.

■ The general collection of Java documentation is available via anonymous FTP at `ftp://java.sun.com/docs/`. In particular `javaspec.ps.gz` is the specification for the Java programming language.

Chapter Summary

Java is a language that brings new possibilities to the Web by making executable content possible. However, at its heart, Java is a programming language, with data declarations, control flow, computational statements, and ways to make methods (functions). Java also adds the ability for a programmer to create applets that "run" through cycles of activity.

■ The framework for Java programs is the class statement. A class is a template for creating instances, or objects, that have the data and methods described in the class definition.

■ Java programs can be applications that run as standalone programs or applets that are interpreted by a HotJava browser.

■ Java data can be declared using types such as integer (`int`), real numbers (`float`), strings (`String`), and true/false values (`boolean`). Java data can be placed in arrays; array indexing starts at 0.

■ Java allows a very flexible way for programmers to create meaningful names for identifiers, methods, and classes.

■ Java supports a range of operators and mathematical expressions for computation and comparison. Mathematical expressions are evaluated following precedence rules for operators. Expressions can also be changed to another data type through casting. For example, a real expression can be converted to a string or to an integer.

■ Flow control statements in Java support branching and looping. Branching is possible with the `if ... else` statement or the `switch ... case` statement. Looping can be done zero or more times using the `while` statement. Looping occurs one or more times using the `do ... while` statement.

- Methods are one of the means in Java to create re-usable code. A method is like a little program unto itself and can contain its own local variables or methods. Rules for determining where a reference to a variable is valid are called scoping rules. Scoping rules help resolve references to a variable within a method if the variable has the same name as class variables.
- Java's Runnable interface allows programmers to create executable pages.
- Appendix B of this book contains quick reference information on the Java language.

CHAPTER 11

Java Is Object-Oriented

The previous chapter showed you the basics of the programming structure and procedural features of Java applications and applets. Because Java is organized by the object-oriented paradigm, its structure involves the class as the basic unit of programming. Even in creating applications, as the previous chapter showed, the class definition is the frame around which you build a Java program.

It would be a mistake, however, to see the class definition as only a framework for programming. To take advantage of the true benefit of object-orientation, you can learn how a class is organized, and how subclasses and objects can be made using this class. In fact, your skills in using existing classes and specializing them to model the world is the important skill to gain as a Java programmer.

This chapter explores the class in Java and shows you how subclasses and objects can be made from a class.

Defining and Using Classes in Java

The examples of classes shown in the previous chapter were indeed true Java classes. However, because they were merely demonstration programs of the procedural aspects of Java, those examples didn't show the true power that comes from organizing software into classes. This section first shows more parts of a class, including different methods and how they work.

An Example Class

A *class* is the basic unit both conceptually and syntactically of a Java program. A Java class describes a set of data and methods that can act upon that data. When an identifier is declared to be of the type defined by a class, that identifier is an *object* of that class. Therefore, a class is like a "template" for generating objects of its type.

You can use classes to model real-world objects. For example, a safe in the real world is an object used to store and protect items so that only people with authorization can obtain them. A simple safe has a locked door with a combination to open the door. The safe can be either locked or unlocked, and you use the combination to unlock the safe. Anyone can look at the outside of the safe and see markings on it (such as a door number) or try the door to see if it is locked. Anyone can also try an arbitrary combination on the safe and check to see if it unlocks the safe. However, only the combination that is designed to open the safe's lock can unlock the safe. Only the creators of the safe can set the lock itself so that it unlocks with a particular combination.

This safe example is a good candidate to model as a Java class. Here is the Java code to the define a safe class. In this code, you'll see some new features that build on the class structure that you saw in the previous chapter.

```
/**
 Program:    Safe Class
 Purpose:    demonstrates a Java Class and protections;
 @author     john@december.com
 @version    1.04; 23 July 1995
 */

class Safe {

    public    int     doorNumber   = 123;
    private   boolean locked       = true;
    private   int     combination  = 456;

    public boolean isLocked(){
        return(locked);
    }

    public void unLock(int thisCombination) {
        if (thisCombination == combination) unLock();
    }

    private void unLock() {
        locked = false;
    }
```

```
   private void setCombination(int setting) {
      combination = setting;
   }

   Safe () { }

   Safe (int door) {
      doorNumber = door;
      setCombination(doorNumber); // this is the trick to cracking a safe
   }

}
```

The first line:

```
class Safe {
```

announces to the Java compiler that this is a class definition. The class gets a name (`Safe`). The rest of the code defines the body of the class.

Data for the *Safe* Class

Here is the data for the `Safe` class:

```
public    int     doorNumber    = 123;
   private  boolean  locked        = true;
   private  int      combination   = 456;
```

There's no requirement to list all the variables at the top of the class, but it is often good programming practice to group them together so that a reader can quickly find out what this class describes. The safe class has three variables:

- ■ `doorNumber` to store the marking on the outside of the safe telling which safe it is. This is an integer and is initialized to a value of `123`. This means that, unless changed elsewhere in the description of the class, an object created of type `Safe` will have a door number `123`. This doesn't mean that this door number is permanent. Because there is no `final` keyword in the declaration of `doorNumber`, it is not a constant.

- ■ `locked` to store the state of the safe: whether it is locked or unlocked. This is modeled very well by a Boolean variable and is initially set to `true`.

- ■ `combination` to store the combination of the safe. With this number, a user of the safe can open it.

Data in a class can be set to have varying levels of access to other classes. In the safe example, it would not be a good idea if just anyone could look at the combination or to be able to easily manipulate the variable storing the safe's status as locked or unlocked. Therefore, both the variables `locked` and `combination` are set to be `private` data for this class. This means that these variables can never be examined or altered outside the class description. Objects declared to be type `Safe` won't be able to be "tricked" into revealing the combination or opening the safe without the right combination. Because the door number is something that anyone can see anyway, it is `public` making this variable freely readable (and writeable) through objects declared type `Safe`.

Methods of the *Safe* Class

The methods that operate on the Safe class data include a full range of activities outlined in the real-world narrative describing what a safe should do:

- public boolean isLocked(): This method allows any user (public access to this method) to check to see if the safe is locked or unlocked. The body of this method reveals the value of the private variable locked. This is the only way a user can find out if a safe is locked or not.

- public void unLock(int thisCombination): This method checks to see if the combination passed in the parameter list (thisCombination) matches the safe's actual combination. Because anyone can try a combination on the safe, this is a public method. If the combination matches, the safe is unlocked with the private method unLocked.

- private void unLock(): This method alters the value of the locked variable. This is a private method, so it can only be referenced in the body of the class definition.

- private void setCombination(int setting): This method alters the value of the combination variable. Because not anyone should be able to set this variable, this method is declared private.

Every time you create an object of type Safe, a special method called a constructor is executed. A constructor has the same name as its class and it does not return a value. All constructors are public, so it is not possible to make one private. The constructor

```
Safe () { }
```

doesn't do anything for a new safe except create it. The constructor also makes the initializations of the variables declared: doorNumber = 123;, locked = true;, and combination = 456;. The programmer could have placed these initializations in the body of the Safe() constructor. You can create a new object of type Safe in another class or application with this constructor like this:

```
Safe aSafe = new Safe();
```

The Safe class has another constructor:

```
Safe (int door) {
   doorNumber = door;
   setCombination(doorNumber);  // this is the trick to cracking a safe
}
```

This constructor allows you to create an object of type Safe, which has a specific value for doorNumber. This value is passed as a parameter. The fact that there are two constructors means that the method Safe in the class is *overloaded*. Using this second constructor, you can create a safe with door number 1927:

```
Safe anotherSafe = new Safe(1927);
```

The Java language can figure out which one of the two constructors to call because the two constructors have different parameter lists:

The Safe(1927) reference would call the second constructor listed in the class. Notice also that this constructor contains the "trick" that can be used to unlock any safe: you can use the door number as the combination. Of course, this is a very poor security feature, but it will illustrate the Safe class well.

You can visualize the Safe class as in figure 11.1. A safe's protected data and methods, including the combination and door status and the ability to manipulate these are "hidden" and protected inside its outer shell of public methods.

Figure 11.1.
A visualization of the
Safe *class.*

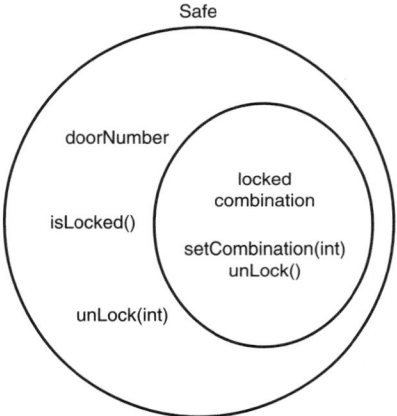

Using the *Safe* Class

The preceding Safe class is a good, simple model of a real-world safe. However, the code itself, a class declaration, isn't directly executable. Using the Java compiler, you can compile the file containing the class definition:

```
$ javac Safe.java
```

This will create a file called Safe.class containing the bytecodes for this class. But there is nothing more you can do with just that file alone. Trying to run it in the Java interpreter will yield an error:

```
In class Safe: void main(String argv[]) is not defined
```

The class Safe does not contain the designation extends Applet in its declaration, so it won't work as an applet on a web page. Instead, you can use classes like Safe in Java in classes, in applications, and in applets.

For example, a programmer can create an application to create and use objects of type Safe to simulate a game. In this game, the programmer tries to "crack" safes. Here is such an application:

```
/**
Program:    SpyGame Class for application
Purpose:    demonstrates features of class Safe;
@author     john@december.com
@version    1.07; 23 July 1995
*/

class SpyGame {

    public static void main (String args[]) {

        System.out.println("SpyGame application...");

        Safe theSafe = new Safe();

        System.out.println("Which safe is this? " + theSafe.doorNumber);
        System.out.println("Is the safe locked? " + theSafe.isLocked());

        /* Try to unlock the safe with a guessed combination of 999: */
        theSafe.unLock(999);

        System.out.println("Is 999 the combination? " + theSafe.isLocked());

        /* This wont' work:  theSafe.unLock();
           Gives compiler error: "Method void unLock() in class
           Safe is not accessible from class SpyGame."  */

        /* How about stealing the combination?
           Reference to this won't work:  theSafe.combination;
           Gives compiler error: "Variable combination in class Safe not
           accessible from class SpyGame."  */

        /* How about resetting the safe's lock to a known combination?
           This won't work:  theSafe.setCombination(999);
           Gives compiler error: "Method void setCombination(int) in class
           Safe is not accessible from class SpyGame." */

        /* How about defacing the door's number? */
        System.out.println("Changing the door number ...");
        theSafe.doorNumber = 555;
        System.out.println("Now the door is number: " + theSafe.doorNumber);
        theSafe.unLock(theSafe.doorNumber);
        System.out.println("Is the safe locked? " + theSafe.isLocked());

        System.out.println("However, you can crack your own safe ...");

        Safe mySafe = new Safe(999);

        System.out.println("Is my safe locked? " + mySafe.isLocked());
        System.out.println("My safe has door number " + mySafe.doorNumber);

        System.out.println("Unlocking safe with combination as doorNumber...");
        mySafe.unLock(mySafe.doorNumber);

        System.out.println("Is my safe locked now? " + mySafe.isLocked());

    }
}
```

To run the SpyGame application, you have to compile both SpyGame.java and Safe.java. Then you can run SpyGame:

```
$ javac Safe.java
$ javac SpyGame.java
$ java SpyGame
SpyGame application...
Which safe is this? 123
Is the safe locked? true
Is 999 the combination? true
Changing the door number ...
Now the door is number: 555
Is the safe locked? true
However, you can crack your own safe ...
Is my safe locked? true
My safe has door number 999
Unlocking safe with combination as doorNumber...
Is my safe locked now? false
```

Using Subclasses in Java

The preceding example of the safe is very useful for showing how a class is declared and the differences between its public and private data and methods. However, object-oriented programming only begins to take on real power when a programmer defines classes that inherit data and methods from other objects. The examples of applets shown in the previous chapters were actually subclasses of the Java class Applet and inherited many characteristics of that class. By having child classes inherit characteristics from parent classes, a programmer can incrementally extend the power of software without "breaking" previous code. This incremental specialization of parent classes through child classes also permits a more flexible, modular approach to programming.

An Example Class and Subclasses

Creating classes that can be used as parent classes for other classes takes skill in thinking about the problem domain a Java program might address. A class should encapsulate a set of data and methods using that data that "hangs together" in the programmer's mind. The example of the safe shown previously is a good example: the safe class neatly "packages" all the essential features (from the programmer's view) of a safe.

Here is another example class that models part of a dramatic presentation, a segment:

```
/**
 Program:    Segment Class
 Purpose:    demonstrates a Class;
 @author     john@december.com
 @version    1.03; 23 July 1995
 */

class Segment {

    private String thePlace = "Unknown";
    private int segmentNumber;
```

```java
    Segment (int number) {
       segmentNumber = number;
    }

    Segment(int number, String aPlace) {
       this(number);
       thePlace = aPlace;
    }

    public void header() {
       System.out.println("Segment #" + segmentNumber + " " + thePlace);
    }

    public void action() { }

    public void cut() {
       System.out.println("--------------");
    }
}
```

According to this class definition, every segment must have a number, because its constructor methods both include the segment number in their parameter lists; and there is no constructor without any parameters. A segment occurs at a named place that is by default named Unknown if the constructor that identifies the place is not used.

In the body of the second constructor, the first line

```java
this(number);
```

is a reference to the Segment(int number) constructor. The keyword this identifies the Segment class itself and the single integer parameter resolves the reference to the first constructor.

The rest of the methods of the class define particular actions that can be performed on a segment:

- header(): announces the segment number and setting;
- action(): an empty method that does nothing, but which subclasses of Segment inherit and might implement.
- cut(): a method to end the segment.

An object declared to be of type Segment would have only minimal usefulness. But a child class inheriting from Segment will have all of Segment's features already built in. For example, an action segment:

```java
/**
 Program:    Action Class
 Purpose:    demonstrates a child of the Segment Class;
 @author     john@december.com
 @version    1.03; 23 July 1995
 */

class Action extends Segment {

   Action (int number) {
      super(number);
   }
```

```
    Action(int number, String aPlace) {
        super(number, aPlace);
    }

    public void action() {
        opening();
        focus();
    }

    private void opening() {
        System.out.println("flourish");
    }

    public void focus() {
        System.out.println("panorama");
    }
}
```

The Action class is a subclass of the Segment class because of the statement

```
class Action extends Segment
```

The constructors of Action both use references to the special keyword super to let these constructors "fall through" to the constructors for the parent class, Segment. The Action class adds a new action method that calls two private methods, opening and focus.

In addition to making subclasses from them, you can also use classes to create objects in another class. For example, a person class can be defined:

```
/**
 Program:    Person Class
 Purpose:    demonstrates a parent class to create instances;
 @author     john@december.com
 @version    1.05; 23 July 1995
 */

class Person {

    public static int classLines = 0;
    public int instanceLines = 0;

    private String personName = "Unknown";
    private String tagLine = "Unknown";

    Person () { }

    Person (String name) {
        personName = name;
    }

    Person (String name, String line) {
        this(name);
        tagLine = line;
    }

    public void setTagLine (String line) {
        tagLine = line;
```

```
   }

   public String tagLine () {
      return(tagLine);
   }

   public void say(String line) {
      System.out.println(personName + ": " + "\"" + line + "\"");
      classLines++;   // this statement increments the class variable classLines by 1
      instanceLines++;   // this statement increments the instance variable
instanceLines by 1
   }
}
```

A person has a name and a special "tag" line (something that the person characteristically says).
A person can speak (using the method say) a line; or the tag line of that person can be changed
(setTagLine).

This class's data includes two variables, classLines and instanceLines. The first of these is defined as type static making it associated with the class (it can be called a *class* variable). This
means that all objects defined as class Person in a program will *share* this single variable. The
other variable, instanceLines is not declared as static, so it is associated with each *instance* of
this class. Every object declared of type Person will have a separate variable, instanceLines.

The Person class can then be used in another subclass of the Segment class:

```
/**
Program:    Dialogue Class
Purpose:    demonstrates a objects of the PersonClass;
@author     john@december.com
@version    1.03; 23 July 1995
*/

class Dialogue extends Segment {

   private Person personA;
   private Person personB;

   Dialogue (int number) {
      super(number);   // this refers to the constructor for the parent class,
      Segment
   }

   Dialogue(int number, String aPlace) {
      super(number, aPlace);   // this refers to the constructor for the parent
      class, Segment
   }

   Dialogue (int number, String aPlace,
            String actor1Name, String actor2Name) {
      this(number, aPlace);
      personA = new Person(actor1Name);   // this creates a person with a given
      name
      personB = new Person(actor2Name);
   }
```

```java
public void action() {
    greetings();
    talk();
    wrapup();
}

private void greetings() {
    personA.say("Hi");
    personB.say("Hello");
    personA.setTagLine("Gosh, it is Hot");
    personB.setTagLine("Yup");
}

private void talk() {
    personA.say(personA.tagLine());
    personB.say(personB.tagLine());
    personA.say(personA.tagLine());
}

private void wrapup() {
    personA.say("Bye");
    personB.say("See ya");
    System.out.println(personA.classLines);
    System.out.println(personA.instanceLines);
    System.out.println(personB.classLines);
    System.out.println(personB.instanceLines);
}
}
```

This class, Dialogue, is a subclass of Segment and uses the Person class to make the actors to take part in the dialogue. Similar to the Action class, the Dialogue class uses the super keyword to make its constructors "fall through" to its parent's class. Dialogue also has a special constructor that takes an additional two parameters: names of two actors to take part in the dialogue. This constructor makes new people with these names for the dialogue:

```java
personA = new Person(actor1Name);
personB = new Person(actor2Name);
```

These people are data for the Segment and are used in the methods greetings, talk, and wrapup for creating dialogue.

All the objects can now be used in an application to showcase what they can do:

```java
/**
Program:     Drama Class
Purpose:     demonstrates objects and classes;
@author      john@december.com
@version     1.06; 18 July 1995
*/

class Drama{

    public static void main (String args[]) {

        System.out.println("Drama application...");

        Dialogue afternoon = new Dialogue (1, "back at the office",
                            "Kyle", "Georgie");
```

```
        afternoon.header();
        afternoon.action();
        afternoon.cut();

        Action night = new Action (2, "city streets");
        night.header();
        night.action();
        night.cut();

    }
}
```

The classes can be compiled and run:

```
$ javac Segment.java
$ javac Person.java
$ javac Dialogue.java
$ javac Action.java
$ javac Drama.java
$ java Drama
Drama application...
Segment #1 back at the office
Kyle: "Hi"
Georgie: "Hello"
Kyle: "Gosh, it is Hot"
Georgie: "Yup"
Kyle: "Gosh, it is Hot"
Kyle: "Bye"
Georgie: "See ya"
7
4
7
3
-------------
Segment #2 city streets
flourish
panorama
-------------
```

Notice that the numbers at the end of segment one show the value for the variables classLines and instanceLines for both Kyle and Georgie:

```
System.out.println(personA.classLines);
     System.out.println(personA.instanceLines);
     System.out.println(personB.classLines);
     System.out.println(personB.instanceLines);
```

Kyle spoke four lines and Georgie said three. Both Kyle and Georgie's class variable classLines was set to the total number of lines all persons in the dialogue said.

Java is a *late-bound* language. This means that methods can be added to a class such as Segment without having to recompile its child classes (unless, of course, the child class is altered to take advantage of the new parent methods).

Chapter Summary

The examples of the classes used in this chapter show the very basic pieces that a Java programmer needs to put together to form powerful Java applications and applets. Making and using classes and subclasses and objects is the key to taking advantage of the object-oriented nature of Java.

- Classes are the basic building blocks of a Java program. A class is a template for creating objects that have data and methods associated with them.
- Data and methods of a class can be hidden from other classes by the keyword `private` or made accessible with the keyword `public` in their declarations.
- Special methods called constructors in a class are automatically executed every time an object is created of the class type.
- Several methods in a class can have the same name as long as they differ in their parameter lists. This is called overloading.
- The keyword `extends` in a class declaration identifies it as a subclass. A subclass inherits its parent's class non-private data and methods.
- Subclasses can refer to their parent class with the keyword `super`; classes can refer to themselves with the keyword `this`.
- Objects can be created of a class type by using the `new` keyword before the name of the class constructor.
- Variables declared using the keyword `static` in a class are shared with all objects in a program of that class type.
- Subclasses and classes can be used in applications to create software that is understandable, reliable, and extensible.
- Appendix B of this book contains references to more online sources of information about Java and object-oriented programming.

pplet Development Involves Design and Implementation

The Java applications you saw in the previous two chapters showed some basics of programming in the Java language. Chapter 10 reviewed the fundamentals of what a Java programmer needs to know about Java's procedural aspects; Chapter 11 examined the object-oriented nature of Java, including how to use classes to create objects or subclasses. As a programmer, however, you need to know still more: how to develop effective programs using design strategies that take both user interface issues as well as software reliability and understandability considerations into account.

Java, like any other programming language or even human language, is expressive and makes possible many choices for organizing information. This wide range of choices makes the task of using Java to create applets a challenging one. This chapter surveys applet development, focusing on considerations for design and implementation. After some general considerations about applets and design, this chapter presents a full case study of a `Runnable` applet, which uses several classes and illustrates Java design and implementation issues.

Thinking About Applets

A Java applet can be a simple animation, like Duke tumbling across the screen, or support a framework for user interaction and activity such as the spreadsheet (refer to Chapter 1). In designing applets, you need to consider what the work of that applet should be and how it will accomplish this work for its intended users on the Web. A Java applet involves more than just the code that implements computation and display. A Java applet is also an expression of a user interface. As a Java programmer, you can thus consider who will use the applet and why.

In thinking about an applet, a Java developer can consider:

- **Audience:**

  Who is the intended audience of the applet?

  Why will they use the applet?

  What is their level of knowledge of the problem domain the applet addresses?

  What is their level of experience with information on the Web that presents the applet?

- **Purpose:**

  What kind of activity does the applet support? This might include supporting information, communication, or interaction.

  What is the expected outcome of using the applet? This might include education or entertainment.

- **Design Issues:**

  What is the information context in which this applet appears? How does this applet support or augment this larger context?

  What interface paradigm might best support user needs? For example, the crossword puzzle applet earlier in this book very nicely supports a paradigm that matches the user experience of this game on paper. This paradigm can reinforce the user's actions to perceive, select, and interact with the applet.

  How can the interaction offered by the applet be broken up into units of perception and response? These units may influence the creation of classes and a class hierarchy.

Design is not a simple task, particularly when there are so many choices possible. The Web's hypermedia supports a wide range of possibilities for user perception and selection. Applets provide ways for richer forms of interactivity to be part of the Web.

Designing an Applet

To illustrate some of the considerations in applet design and implementation, consider this example application description:

> Design an applet that simulates events of a scene from a play on a Web page. A scene involves actors who deliver lines during the scene based on a script.

An approach to designing an applet for this situation might be:

- **Identify the classes.** The nouns in the problem description are often excellent candidates for classes. The nouns: events, scene, actor, and script identify important parts of the application. A class can be thought of as "anything that you can draw a box around" in the sense that a class can be anything as long as it can be distinguished from what it is not. A class's data and its operations upon that data need to be defined. Often, the verbs in the application description can give a good clue as to methods that might be defined in the classes.

- **Determine class relationships.** Figure 12.1 summarizes how a scene has a series of events; these events involve the actors and a script.

Figure 12.1.
Class relationships.

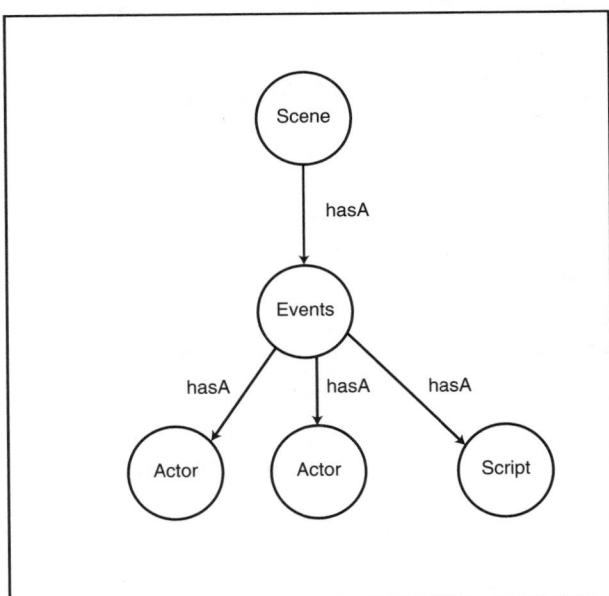

- **Determine class responsibilities.** A good class structure takes advantage of possibilities for generalization and specialization. Generalization is a way to encapsulate what is common among objects to a single parent class. Specialization is taking a parent class and making its child do a particular task by adding more specialized functionality. Ideally, a class structure would make both directions possible and give a programmer just the right class to use in an application without ever having to duplicate functionality.

■ **Identify methods and data.** The methods and data give a class its unique characteristics. As you saw in the previous examples, the methods determine how objects created from a class can be manipulated. Only `public` methods and data are available for use by any other classes.

■ **Scene.** This class will need to be a subclass of `Applet` and implement `Runnable` in order to support an "animated" web page. Its public methods include the methods for `Runnable` classes. Its private data can include an object of type `Events` and `Thread`.

■ **Events.** An object of this class will be used by the `Scene` class to manage the composition and flow of events in the scene. Public methods it should respond to include a method to get the next event and to check for more events to see if the scene is over. Private data includes constants to set the arrangement of the display, a script object, and two actor objects.

■ **Actor.** An actor needs to say lines, and be placed and displayed in the scene.

■ **Script.** This class needs to hold the title and lines of the play.

Implementing an Applet

The preceding design identifies the pieces that will make up the applet. The `Scene` class is the "root" class of interest, and the other classes support it. The implementation of `Scene` closely follows the model of the `EssentialRunner` shown in Chapter 11:

```
import browser.Applet;
import awt.Graphics;
/**
 Program:    Scene class
 Purpose:    applet that implements a scene of activity
 @author     john@december.com
 @version    1.99; 23 Jul 1995
*/

class Scene extends Applet implements Runnable {

    static int sceneWidth  = 500;
    static int sceneHeight = 500;

    private Thread flow;
    private Events action;    // see the class definition for Events
    private boolean done = false;
    private boolean pause = false;

    public void init() {
        resize(sceneWidth, sceneHeight);
    }
```

```
public void start() {
    if (flow == null) {
        flow = new Thread(this);
        flow.start();
    }
    action = new Events();
}

public void paint(Graphics context) {
    context.clearRect(0, 0, sceneWidth, sceneHeight);
    action.nextEvent();
    action.paint(context);
    done = (action.moreEvents() == false);
}

public void update() {
    repaint();
}

public void run() {
    try {
        while (!done) {
            if (!pause) repaint();
        }
    }
}

public void stop() {
    done = true;
    if (flow.isAlive()) flow.stop();
    flow = null;
}

public void mouseDown(int x, int y) {
    pause = !pause;
}
}
```

The Scene class is basically the skeleton of the code that makes the applet on the page a Runnable applet. The key method in its operation is the main method, which continually loops and re-paints the display area as long as the user has not clicked the mouse to pause the activity. Figure 12.2 shows a graphical depiction of the Scene class. The class itself is depicted as a large circle with its public methods and data shown on the outer edge of the circle. The methods are identified by the () symbol following their names. Inside the larger class circle is another circle enclosing the private portion of the class.

The diagram also shows relationships to other classes: Scene is a subclass of (extends) Applet and implements the interface Runnable. Scene's private data includes the object flow, which is a Thread object, and action, which is an Events object.

The Events class is a central organizer for setting up the scene and stepping through it. Its private data includes two actors and constants for arranging text on the screen and a pause method. Figure 12.3 shows a graphical representation of Events and its relationships to the Script and Actor classes.

Figure 12.2.
The Scene class.

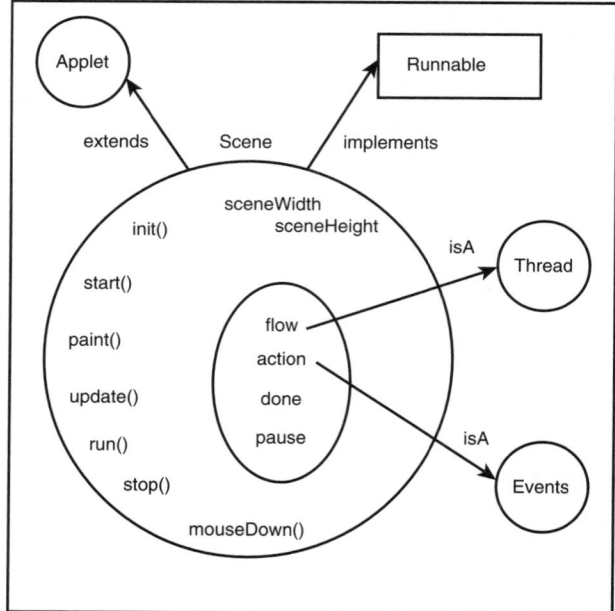

Figure 12.3.
The Events class.

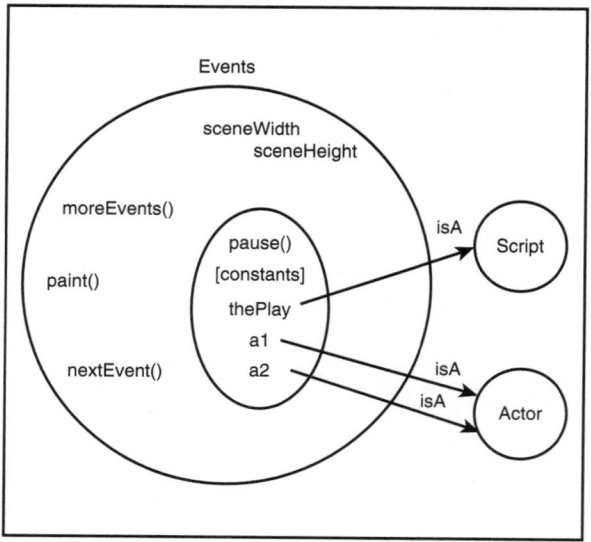

This is an implementation of Events:

```
import awt.Graphics;
/**
 Program:    Events class
 Purpose:    a class which executes all the events
 @author     john@december.com
```

```
@version    1.56; 23 Jul 1995
*/

class Events {

    private final int OVER = 999;        // All events over
    private final int MORE = 0;          // More events still to come

    private final int HIGHDRAMA   = 10;  // long, dramatic pauses
    private final int MEDIUMDRAMA =  5;  // medium pauses
    private final int LOWDRAMA    =  1;  // short pauses

    private final int MIDDLE = 150;      // stage location
    private final int FRONT  = 200;      // stage location
    private final int BACK   = 100;      // stage location
    private final int eventInterval = 200;

    private int status = MORE;
    private Script thePlay;
    private Actor a1, a2;

    Events() {
        // The script and characters are created and placed on the stage.
        thePlay = new Script("The Time Bandits");
        a1 = new Actor("Ann", 5, 100, MIDDLE);
        a2 = new Actor("Bob", 5, 100, FRONT);
    }

    public boolean moreEvents() {
        return (!(status == OVER));
    }

    private void pause(int drama) {
        Thread.sleep(eventInterval*drama);
    }

    public void paint(Graphics context){
        a1.paint(context);
        a2.paint(context);
        pause(MEDIUMDRAMA);
    }

    public void nextEvent() {
        a1.say(thePlay.getLine(Actor.actorLines));
        a2.say(thePlay.getLine(Actor.actorLines));
        if (thePlay.doneScript(Actor.actorLines)) status = OVER;
    }
}
```

The Actor class can be implemented by a set of fairly simple methods to display lines and position these lines in the display area. Here is an implementation:

```
import awt.Graphics;
/*
 Program:    Actor class
 Purpose:    an actor for plays
 @author     john@december.com
 @version    1.51; 23 July 1995
 */

class Actor {
```

```
//-- Class variable
static int actorLines = 0;              // lines all actors have said

//-- Private variables
private int lineCount = 0;              // number of lines this actor has said
private int stagePosition = 0;          // where actor's lines appear
private int leftMargin = 0;             // left margin for actor's name
private int lineMargin = 0;             // left margin for actor's spoken lines
private String actorName = "?";         // actor's stage name
private String nextLine = "?";          // the actor's next utterance

//-- Constructors

Actor () { }                            // minimum actor creation

Actor (String name) {
   actorName = name;
}

Actor (String name, int left, int line, int position) {  // max actor creation
   actorName = name;
   leftMargin = left;
   lineMargin = line;
   stagePosition = position;
}

//-- Methods

public void paint(Graphics context){
   context.drawString(actorName, leftMargin, stagePosition);
   context.drawString(nextLine, lineMargin, stagePosition);
}

public void setMargins(int left, int line){
   leftMargin = left;
   lineMargin = line;
}

public void setPosition(int position){
   stagePosition = position;
}

public int linesSaid(){
   return (lineCount);
}

public void say(String line) {
   nextLine = line;
   lineCount++;
   actorLines++;
}
}
```

Figure 12.4 shows a graphical depiction of the Actor class.

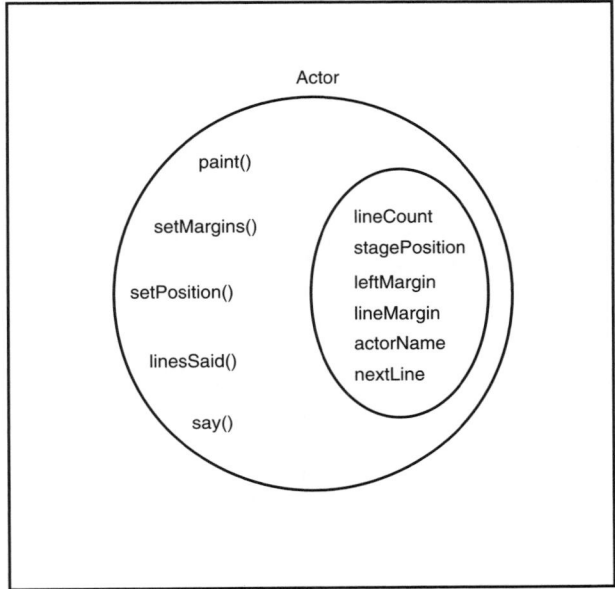

Figure 12.4.
The Actor *class.*

The Script class is very simple: it is merely a holder for the lines of the play:

```
/**
 Program:    Script object
 Purpose:    contains lines for script
 @author     john@december.com
 @version    1.05; 23 Jul 1995
 */

class Script {

   private String scriptTitle;

   Script () { }

   Script (String title) {
      scriptTitle = title;
   }

   public boolean doneScript(int line){
      return (line == scriptLines.length);
   }

   public String getTitle(){
      return (scriptTitle);
   }

   public String getLine(int line){
      return (scriptLines[line]);
   }
```

```
private String scriptLines[] = {
    "Hi.",
    "Hi there.",
    "What time is it?",
    "Now.",
    "This is silly.",
    "How much?",
    "Too much.",
    "And so?",
    "So what.",
    "I have to go."};
}
```

Figure 12.5 shows a graphical depiction of the Script class.

Figure 12.5.
The Script class.

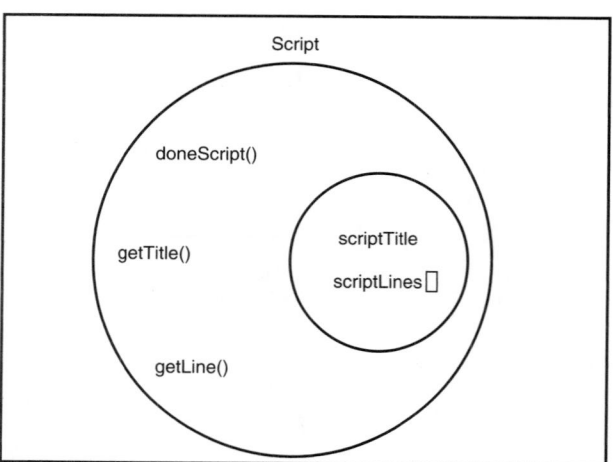

A programmer can now set up an HTML page like this:

```
<HTML>
<HEAD>
   <TITLE>Scene Design Applet</TITLE>
</HEAD>
<BODY>
   <P>"This is a scene from a play: " <APP Class="Scene">
</BODY>
</HTML>
```

The programmer then compiles all the .java source files and places the resulting .class files in a subdirectory, classes, in the directory in which the HTML page is located. Figure 12.6 shows an example dialogue exchange from the running application. The lines of the dialogue are displayed two at a time, one from each actor, until the actors have said all the lines. The result is, for the user, perhaps something like watching a captioned movie. However, this example application just illustrates the issues involved in design and simple implementation. Using hypermedia, the class for Actor could be made more elaborate: audio files could be added as well as graphics to give an experience for the user.

Figure 12.6.
Dialogue from the scene.

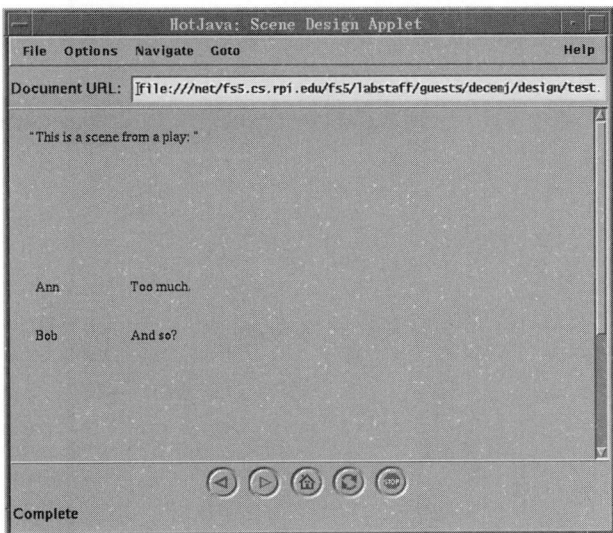

Chapter Summary

Java is an object-oriented programming language that defines the behavior of a Java application. Used in applets, Java classes provide a user interface as well as computation and information processing. Creating an applet involves considering the audience, purpose, and design issues of the problem domain.

- A first step in designing an applet is to write out a statement describing the desired application using terms related to the real-world parts of the problem.

- The next step in design is to identify classes. A class can be anything, but a good class structure requires both generalization and specialization. The nouns in an application description are good candidates to consider for classes.

- Each class in a design should do one thing very well, inheriting data and methods from parent classes where possible, specializing where necessary, and hiding its implementation details from other classes as much as possible through private data and methods. This helps create more modular code that doesn't break when some other software component is changed.

- A designer finally needs to identify the methods and data in the classes that will accomplish the work of the application. Verbs from the application statement are often good starting points for considering which methods must exist.

- Implementing a class involves writing the Java code to describe the data and methods. Graphically, a class can be visualized: its methods and data can be listed and its relationships with other classes defined.

Further Information Sources

This appendix gives you some sources of more online information about Java, the Web, and related topics. When this book was written, Java was in alpha release and was just making its way into more widespread use. This appendix gives you some launching points to find the latest information and updates, as well as some general online reference information.

Java Information Sources

This section gives you links to Java-specific information. These are places to look for the latest updates, as well as more information about this book and Java.

Presenting Java Support Web

To connect to the latest information about this book's contents, open the URL `http://www.rpi.edu/~decemj/works/java.html`. This support web provides links to online information about this book, code samples, updates on resources, and related information. Check with the errata page for corrections, and send reports of other errors, problems, or questions to John December at the Internet address `john@december.com`. For links to more John December book support sites, see `http://www.december.com/works/`.

Major Java Repositories

These are places to get official information about Java and obtain its code distribution:

- **Sun's Main Java Site** (http://java.sun.com/): This is the one-stop, authoritative source for Java information, including Java/HotJava code distribution. Geographically, this server is located on the West Coast of the United States, in the San Francisco Bay area (Mountain View, California). This Web site has a searching feature so that you can quickly find the specific information you need about the latest Java topics. You can download the latest version of the HotJava browser using a click-to-download feature on the distribution page. The Anonymous File Transfer Protocol site for code distribution is at ftp://java.sun.com/.

- **SunSITE at the University of North Carolina** (http://sunsite.unc.edu/java/): This is a mirror of Sun's main Java site. This SunSITE is located in Chapel Hill, North Carolina. Anonymous File Transfer Protocol for information and code distribution at ftp://sunsite.unc.edu/pub/languages/java.

At these Java sites, look for

- The Java FAQ (Frequently Asked Questions) list with answers
- The latest information about bugs, ports, and browsers
- Mailing and discussion list information
- Programmer guides for Java
- User guides for HotJava
- Demonstration applets

Indexes

Because Java is so new, few indexes of Java information exist outside Sun. Once Java becomes more prevalent, however, the Yahoo index (http://www.yahoo.com/) might be a good place to start to look for more information.

- **Yahoo Index** entry for Computers-Languages-Java (http://www.yahoo.com/Computers/Languages/Java/): This is a listing of Java-related information. Growing from links to Sun's Main Java Site, this index eventually should include related unofficial pages of information related to Java.

- **The Wild, Wild World of HotJava** (http://www.science.wayne.edu/~joey/java.html): A listing of information about the HotJava browser, including the latest information on ports. This index is maintained by Joey Oravec.

Java Online Bibliography

This is a list of online articles and key press releases about the Java programming language, the browser HotJava, and related technologies.

- Banks, David. "Why Sun thinks Hot Java will give you a lift." *San Jose Mercury News*, March 23, 1995. URL `http://www.sjmercury.com/archives/hotjava.htm`.

- Karpinski, Richard. "Hot Java arrives: Sun aims to revolutionize the Web." *InteractiveAge*, May 22, 1995. URL `http://techweb.cmp.com/ia/15issue/15hotjava.html`.

- Louis, Tristan. "Java on the Menu: Causing Jitters?" *WebWeek*, June 1995. URL `http://www.mecklerweb.com/ww/news/june-95/paper/df/1-2java.html`.

- Netscape Communications Corporation. "Netscape to License Sun's Java Programming Language." Netscape press release, May 23, 1995. URL `http://home.netscape.com/newsref/pr/newsrelease25.html`.

- O'Connell, Michael. "Java: The Inside Story." *SunWorld Online*, July 1995. URL `http://www.sun.com/sunworldonline/swol-07-1995/swol-07-java.html`.

- Sullivan, Eamonn. "Sun's Java technology perks up WWW." *PC Week Online*, June 5, 1995. URL `http://www.ziff.com:8002/~pcweek/reviews/june_1995/java.html`.

- "Sun Brings True Interactivity To The World Wide Web." *SunFlash*, 77.25, May 1995. `http://www.flashback.com/www/may.1995/sunflash/77.25.www.html`.

- "Sun Launches First Interactive WWW Site Powered By Java." *SunFlash*, 77.27, May 1995. `http://www.flashback.com/www/may.1995/sunflash/77.27.java.html`.

Java-Related Information Sources

You can also learn more about Java by looking at examples of its use and related topics such as object-oriented programming. This section gives you some pointers to organizations who use Java (some of which were discussed in this book), as well as pointers to object-oriented information.

Organizations Using Java

- **Accurate Information Systems** (`http://accurate.com.my/`): This group uses Java in its home page.

- **Dimension X** (`http://www.dimensionx.com/`): A bleeding-edge Internet technology developer. See the work on Iced Java, a 3-D rendering engine.

- **George Coates Performance Works** (`http://www.georgecoates.org/`): A producer of theatrical performances using digital technologies, film, and stage techniques.

- **HotWired** (`http://www.hotwired.com/java/`): This digital version of *Wired* magazine has made some forays into using Java in its user interface.

- **The NandO Times** (`http://www.nando.net/`): This online periodical uses Java in its interface.

- **Netscape Communications** (`http://home.netscape.com/`): This company plans to license Java for use in its Web browsers.

- **Ødegård Labs** (`http://www.odegard.com/`): This a technology developer that uses Java in its Web.

- **The Rolling Stones** (`http://www.stones.com/`):This rock band has a web site demonstrating Java in several pages, including a Java-ized Voodoo Lounge. (See Chapter 4.)

- **Sun Microsystems** (`http://www.sun.com/`): The developers of Java. Sun's corporate Web page includes many examples of applets. In particular, you can use a Java-enabled browser to check out how the icons on the front page change as you pass your cursor over them.

- **VPRO** (`http://www.vpro.nl/`): Public broadcasting from Hilversum, The Netherlands. VPRO uses Java as part of an experimental tour of its web (See Chapter 6).

Object-Oriented Information Sources

- **Object-Oriented Information Sources Index** (`http://cuiwww.unige.ch/OSG/OOinfo/`): A searchable index to a variety of object-oriented information sources, including research groups, archives, companies, books, and bibliographies.

- **Object-Oriented Design Online Reference Guide** (`http://www.clark.net/pub/howie/OO/oo_home.html`): A guide to online information sources regarding object-oriented design. This guide was created by Howie Michalski, Lead Database Engineer, Infrastructure, CompuServe, Inc.

- **Computers—Software—Object-Oriented Programming section from Yahoo** (`http://www.yahoo.com/Computers/Software/Object_Oriented_Programming/`): A general index linking to a variety of object-oriented information sources.

General Web Information

Here are some World Wide Web information sources. You can use these to locate more information about the Web or watch for new applications or browsers for Java.

- **Web overview/W³C** (`http://www.w3.org/`): An overview of the Web, from the World Wide Web Consortium.

- **Web info/EARN** (`http://www.earn.net/gnrt/www.html`): A narrative introducing and explaining the Web from the European Academic Research Network Association (EARN).

- **Web Guide/Hughes** (`http://www.eit.com/web/www.guide/guide.toc.html`): "Entering the World-Wide Web, A Guide to Cyberspace," by Kevin Hughes. See also, Hughes' paper, "From Webspace to Cyberspace" at `http://www.eit.com/~kevinh/cspace/`.

- **Web-Yahoo** (`http://www.yahoo.com/Computers/World_Wide_Web/`): The Computers—World Wide Web section from the popular Yahoo index.

Web FAQs

- **Web FAQ/Boutell** (`http://sunsite.unc.edu/boutell/faq/www_faq.html`): Frequently Asked Questions (FAQ) list and answers about the Web. This FAQ, which is maintained by Thomas Boutell, covers user, provider, and general information.

- **Web FAQ/W³C** (`http://www.w3.org/hypertext/WWW/FAQ/List.html`): Frequently Asked Questions on W³; this list is maintained by Tim Berners-Lee.

Access to the Web

- **Web via e-mail** (`mailto: agora@mail.w3.org Body: www` *URL*): You can obtain a Web file via e-mail. For instructions, send the message body HELP to agora@mail.w3.org.

- **Web via telnet** (`telnet://telnet.w3.org`): You can access the Web via telnet. This is an example of using the Web on the World Wide Web Consortium's computer, `telnet.w3.org`.

- **Web ftp info** (`ftp://ftp.w3.org/pub/www/`): Information files about the Web from CERN; it includes papers, guides, and draft specifications.

- **Web gopher info** (`gopher://gopher.w3.org`): Information files about the Web available via gopher.

- **Bootstrap info** (`http://www.w3.org/hypertext/WWW/FAQ/Bootstrap.html`): Information about learning more about the Web and accessing it.

Web Software

Here are some places to look for new Web browsers and software.

- **Web Clients** (`http://www.w3.org/hypertext/WWW/Clients.html`): A list of programs (Web browsers) from CERN that enable you to access the Web.

- **Web Browsers/Yahoo** (`http://www.yahoo.com/Computers/World_Wide_Web/Browsers/`): A list from Yahoo, Computers—World Wide Web—Browsers.

- **Web Browser source** (`ftp://ftp.w3.org/pub/www/bin/`): A source code for a variety of Web browsers for different hardware platforms.

- **Web Servers** (`http://www.w3.org/hypertext/WWW/Daemon/Overview.html`): A list of programs (Web servers) from CERN that enable you to provide information on the Web.

- **EIT WSK** (`http://wsk.eit.com/wsk/doc/`): Enterprise Integration Technologies Corporation's Webmaster's Starter Kit, a resource to help you install a Web server and optional extensions.

- **Web Software** (`http://www.w3.org/hypertext/WWW/Status.html`): A list of software products related to the Web.

Developing Web Information

- **Web Vlib** (`http://www.stars.com/Vlib`): The Web Development section from the Web Virtual library, a resource collection for Web information providers and users; this information includes general information and links to various resources.

- **HTML Writer's Guild** (`http://www.mindspring.com/~guild/`): An association of HTML writers and Web developers that formed for the purpose of building awareness of Web development skills.

General Internet Information

- **Information Sources: the Internet and Computer-Mediated Communication** (`http://www.rpi.edu/Internet/Guides/decemj/icmc/top.html`): A listing of information sources about the Internet, including technologies, applications, culture, discussion forums, and bibliographies.

- **Internet Web Text** (`http://www.rpi.edu/Internet/Guides/decemj/text.html`): A listing of Internet orientation, searches, exploration, and other resources.

- **Yahoo-Internet** (`http://www.yahoo.com/Computers/Internet/`): The Internet index listing from Yahoo includes a very wide range of sites on many topics.

Java Language Reference

This appendix gives you a quick summary of basic Java language features. Note that this is Java's alpha release; see this book's support site at the URL given in Appendix A for updates.

Java Language Summary

Part IV of this book reviewed some of the basics of programming in Java. This section provides a quick summary of Java for reference.

Classes

A class is the basic organization unit of Java. A class is defined using the class statement and contains data and methods. These data and methods can be hidden from use by other classes (private) or available for reference by other classes (public). Methods in the class that have the same name as the class are called *constructors*.

Any methods in a class can have the same name if they have a different parameter list. Resolution of any name ambiguity is done through matching the number and type of the parameter lists.

A *class* is a template for creating objects of that class type. In a Java program, a programmer creates an object (myObject) of a class ExampleClass, like this:

```
ExampleClass myObject = new ExampleClass();
```

Here is a typical class, showing data and methods, both public and private:

```
/**
 Program:    Safe Class
 Purpose:    demonstrates a Java Class and protections;
 @author     john@december.com
 @version    1.04; 23 July 1995
 */

class Safe {

    public    int     doorNumber   = 123;
    private   boolean locked       = true;
    private   int     combination  = 456;

    public boolean isLocked(){
       return(locked);
    }

    public void unLock(int thisCombination) {
       if (thisCombination == combination) unLock();
    }

    private void unLock() {
       locked = false;
    }

    private void setCombination(int setting) {
       combination = setting;
    }

    Safe() { }

    Safe(int door) {
       doorNumber = door;
       setCombination(doorNumber);  // this is the trick to cracking a safe
    }

}
```

Programmers can create subclasses of a class by using the keyword extends in the class declaration:

```
class StrongBox extends Safe {

    /* rest of subclass definition here */

}
```

A subclass inherits the public methods and data of its parent class. The method by the same name as the class is always public and is called a constructor. A class can have several methods by the same name, as long as the parameter lists differ by parameter types, number of parameters, or order of parameter types.

The keyword this is a reference in a class definition to itself. The keyword super in a subclass definition is a reference to its parent class.

Applications

A Java application is a program that can execute with the Java interpreter (java), outside of the HotJava browser. The HotJava browser itself is a Java application.

Here is a simple application that creates and manipulates an object of the type Safe:

```
/**
 Program:    SpyGame Class for application
 Purpose:    demonstrates features of Safe class;
 @author     john@december.com
 @version    1.08a; 30 July 1995
*/
class SpyGame {
   public static void main (String args[]) {
      Safe mySafe = new Safe(999);
      System.out.println("Is my safe locked? " + mySafe.isLocked());
      System.out.println("My safe has door number " + mySafe.doorNumber);
      mySafe.unLock(mySafe.doorNumber);
      System.out.println("Is my safe locked now? " + mySafe.isLocked());
   }
}
```

Applets

A Java applet is a program that is intended to be observed in the HotJava browser. An applet is a subclass of the Java class Applet. Here is a minimal applet with the source file name HelloWorld.java:

```
import browser.Applet;
import awt.Graphics;

class EssentialApplet extends Applet {
   public void init() {
      resize(600, 300);
   }
   public void paint(Graphics context) {
      context.drawString("Hello, world!", 50, 100);
   }
}
```

An applet is compiled with the Java compiler, javac, producing a class file (for example, HelloWorld.class).

An applet is included in an HTML file through the APP element. Here is the general syntax of an APP element:

```
<APP Class     = "ClassName"
     Src       = "URL or path to directory containing classes directory"
     Align     = "bottom | middle | top"
     Width     = "widthInPixels"
     Height    = "heightInPixels"
AppletSpecificAttribute = "aValue"
     >
```

Here is an example HTML file which includes the HelloWorld applet:

```
<HTML>
<HEAD>
    <TITLE>First Hello Applet</TITLE>
</HEAD>
<BODY>
    <P>"This is it!" <APP Class="EssentialApplet">
</BODY>
</HTML>
```

The class file HelloWorld.class is placed in a subdirectory called classes. This subdirectory is in the directory containing the HTML file.

Interfaces

An *interface* is a collection of methods with the bodies unimplemented. Classes can use the keyword implements and then the interface name; individual classes then can implement the bodies of the methods.

For example:

```
public interface Commerce {
    void public takeOrder(Customer c);
    void public thank(Customer c);
}

public class Store implements Commerce {

    void public takeOrder(Customer person) {
        fulfill(person.desire);
    }

    void public thank(Customer person) {
        person.accept(say("thanks"));
    }
}
```

Packages

A *package* is a collection of classes and/or interfaces. Packages are used to organize the namespace in Java programs. A package is identified by the keyword package as the first non-comment, non-white keyword in the code file:

```
package packageName;
```

Files that do not have a package statement at the start are placed in the default package.

By convention, packages are often named with a prefix set to the author's organization name. After this prefix, the name consists of qualifier words separated by periods.

In another file, a named package can be brought into the namespace by:

```
import packageName;
```

Within a class, method names in packages can be explicitly referenced using the period notation to relieve any ambiguity in names.

Consider an import statement:

```
import webex.project.*;
```

The set of packages with names starting with webex.project may have the same method name, so the dot notation can be used. For example, if the packages webex.project.alpha and webex.project.beta both had a class named List, then they can be referred to as

```
Orders thursday = new webex.project.alpha.List();
Orders friday   = new webex.project.beta.List();
```

The compiled class files of the packages are organized in a directory structure that parallels the dot notation used to refer to the packages.

Bug in Alpha HotJava

A bug in the alpha release of HotJava won't let the browser recognize changes you've made to applets if you restart HotJava in the classes subdirectory. Check to see the latest on this bug at the Sun Microsystems, site at http://java.sun.com/.

Protocol Handlers

- Create the code for the handler as a class named Handler in a file named Handler.java in a package named net.www.protocol.*name*, where *name* is the name of the new protocol.
- Compile the handler, and then place its class file in a subdirectory net/www/protocol/*name* in the classes directory identified in the CLASSPATH environment variable.
- After restarting the browser, it will recognize *run:* URLs.

Content Handlers

- Create the code for the handler as a class named *subtype* in a file named *subtype*.java in a package named net.www.content.*type*, where *type* is the MIME type (see the MIME type table at the end of this appendix) of the new format and *subtype* is the subtype. For example, the type could be text and the subtype could be plain.
- Compile the code, and then place its class file in a subdirectory net/www/content/*type* in the classes directory identified in the CLASSPATH environment variable.
- After restarting the browser, it will interpret files of the format type *subtype*.

Exceptions

An *exception* is an error in a Java program that would cause the program to terminate. Programmers can use the exception handling features of Java to allow the program to die gracefully or recover.

There are exceptions built into the language; see the latest language specifications for a list of these. The programmer can define a new exception:

```
class ProgrammerDefinedException extends Exception {
    /* definition goes here */
}
```

A Java programmer puts an exception handler into the code using the try...catch statements.

```
try {
    result = sum / 0;
} catch (ArithmeticException exception) {
    System.out.println("can't divide by 0!");
} catch (ProgrammerDefinedException exception) {
    System.out.println("some other error");
```

Java Language Information

When you write a program in Java, you'll have to follow the specification for the language. This section summarizes key information about Java language syntax.

The Latest Information

The very latest specification information for Java is available at Sun's Java site. You can check the documentation listings at http://java.sun.com/documentation.html. The specification for the alpha 3 release of Java is available from Sun's main Java site:

http://java.sun.com/1.0alpha3/doc/javaspec/javaspec_1.html

Man pages for all Java software are also available. For example, the alpha 3 man pages are available at

http://java.sun.com/1.0alpha3/doc/man/index.html

As part of its validation service (http://www.halsoft.com/html-val-svc/), HaLSoft offers a HotJava Data Type Definition at http://www.halsoft.com/sgml/HotJava/DTD-HOME.html. This is useful for checking HTML files for proper applet syntax.

Java Reserved Keywords

abstract	boolean	break	byte	byvalue
case	catch	char	class	const
continue	default	do	double	else

extends	false	final	finally	float
for	goto	if	implements	import
instanceof	int	interface	long	native
new	null	package	private	protected
public	return	short	static	super
switch	synchronized	this	threadsafe	throw
transient	true	try	void	while

Permitted Characters

The characters in a Java program can be any Unicode character that is not a reserved character. Unicode is a character-coding standard that can support many world languages. For more information about Unicode, see `http://www.stonehand.com/unicode.html`.

Reserved Characters

These characters are used as operators or separators and therefore can't be used in an identifier name:

```
+  -  !  %  ^  &  *  ¦  ~  /  >

(  )  {  }  [  ]  ;  ?  :  ,  .  =
```

These combinations of characters are used as operators:

```
++ -- == <= != << >>
>>> += -= *= /= &=¦=
^= %=<<= >>= >>>= ¦¦ &&
```

If a special character needs to be represented in a string, use the following table:

Special Codes for Characters

character	*code*
continuation of line	\
new-line NL (LF)	\n
horiztonal tab HT	\t
back space BS	\b
carriage return CR	\r
form feed FF	\f
backslash	\\
single quote	\'
double quote	\"

Java Data Types

- Numeric
  - Integer
    - `byte` 8 bits
    - `short` 16 bits
    - `int` 32 bits
    - `long` 64 bits
  - Floating Point
    - `float` 32 bits (single precision)
    - `double` 64 bits (double precision)
- Character
  - `char` 16 bit unsigned integer set to Unicode character number (this list is available at `ftp://unicode.org/pub/MappingTables/`)
- Logical (boolean)
  - `boolean` has value `true` or `false`
- Arrays
  - identified in a declaration with `[ ]`; created with `new`. Example:

  `int myNumbers[] = new int[40];`

Java Operators

Operator	Use	Example
`[ ]`	array element value	`scores[42]`
`( )`	grouping operator	`counter + (2*3)`
`++`	increment by 1	`counter++` (use, then increment)
`++`	increment by 1	`++counter` (increment, then use)
`--`	decrement by 1	`counter--` (use, then decrement)
`--`	decrement by 1	`--counter` (decrement, then use)
`!`	logical negation	`!done` (true if the value of done is `false`)
`~`	bitwise complement	`~register` (changes 0's to 1's in bit representation)
`instanceof`	is an object of class	`mySafe instanceof Safe`
`*`	multiplication	`4*3` is 12
`/`	division	`7/2` is 3
`%`	modulo (remainder on division)	`35%3` is 2

Operator	Use	Example
+	addition	42+3 is 45
-	subtraction or unary negation	42-3 is 39
<<	left shift	<<register
>>	right shift	>>register
>>>>	zero-fill right shift	>>>>register
<	less than	3 < 42 is true
>>	greater than	3 > 42 is false
<=	less than or equal to	42 <= 42 is true
>>=	greater than or equal to	45 >= 45 is true
==	is equal to	counter==42
!=	is not equal to	counter!=MAXIMUM
&	logical and	a&b(a and b must both be true)
^	exclusive or	a^b (exactly one of the boolean expressions a or b can be true (not both))
¦	inclusive or	a¦b (one of the boolean expressions a or b must be true (possibly both))
&&	logical and; right hand not evaluated	a&&b(a and b must both be true)
¦¦	inclusive or; right hand not evaluated	a¦¦b (one of the boolean expressions a or b must be true (possibly both))
?:	if then	done?say("bye"):say ("continue");
=	assignment	counter = 42;
op=	operator assignment shortcut	counter += 42; add 42 to counter

MIME Types

RFC1521 and RFC1522 specify the types and subtypes for Multipurpose Internet Mail Extensions (MIME). See also (http://ds.internic.net/rfc/rfc1521.txt) and (http://ds.internic.net/rfc/rfc1522.txt), and (ftp://ftp.isi.edu/in-notes/iana/assignments/media-types/).

The x- prefix for the content-type indicates that the extension is not considered a standard type and may change or be defined otherwise by other users.

Type	Subtype	Typical File Extensions
text	enriched	
	html	html htm
	plain	txt text
	tab-separated-values	
	richtext	
multipart	alternative	
	appledouble	
	digest	
	header-set	
	mixed	
	parallel	
message	external-body	
	news	
	partial	
	rfc822	
application	activemessage	
	andrew-inset	
	applefile	
	atomicmail	
	commonground	
	cybercash	
	dca-rft	
	dec-dx	
	eshop	
	iges	
	mac-binhex40	hqx
	macwriteii	
	mathematica	
	msword	doc
	news-message-id	
	news-transmission	
	octet-stream	tar dump readme bin uu exe

Type	Subtype	Typical File Extensions
	oda	oda
	pdf	pdf
	postscript	ps eps ai
	remote-printing	
	riscos	
	rtf	rtf
	slate	
	wita	
	wordperfect5.1	
	x-dvi	dvi
	x-pdf	pdf
	x-tar	tar
	x-tex	tex
	x-www-form-urlencoded	
	x-www-pgp-request	
	x-www-pgp-reply	
	x-www-local-exec	
	zip	zip
image	gif	gif
	ief	ief
	jpeg	jpeg jpg jpe
	rgb	rgb
	tiff	tiff tif
	xbm	xbm
	xpm	xpm
	x-xwindowdump	xwd
	x-pict	pict
audio	basic	au snd
	x-aiff	aif aiff aifc
	x-wav	wav
video	mpeg	mpeg mpg mpe
	quicktime	qt mov
	x-msvideo	avi
	x-sgi-movie	movie

HTML Tag References

This appendix provides a quick reference for HTML tags. Note that the HotJava browser doesn't support tags for tables or HTML extensions such as Netscape's for background textures and colors. Check with the latest documentation for the particular Java-enabled browser that you expect your users to have to learn which HTML tags it supports.

Document Structure and Meta Tags

`<HTML></HTML>`	start and end of HTML document
`<HEAD></HEAD>`	document meta-information start and end
`<TITLE></TITLE>`	document title; goes in `HEAD`
`<BASE Href="URL">`	base reference *URL* of document; goes in `HEAD`
`<BODY></BODY>`	content of document displayed by browser
`<!-- comment -->`	comment; not displayed by browser

Anchors

`<A Href="URL">Hotspot</A>`	anchor linking *Hotspot* text to document *URL*
`<A Name="Jump">Text</A>`	anchor with name *Jump* associated with *Text*
`<A Href="URL#Jump">Hotspot</A>`	anchor with jump from *Hotspot* to anchor named *Jump* in document *URL*

Blocks of Text

`<BLOCKQUOTE></BLOCKQUOTE>`	extended quotation
`<UL></UL>`	unordered list (items marked with `<LI>`)
`<OL></OL>`	ordered list (items marked with `<LI>`)
`<MENU></MENU>`	menu list (items marked with `<LI>`)
`<DIR></DIR>`	directory list (items marked with `<LI>`)
`<DL></DL>`	definition list (terms marked with `<DT>`, definitions marked with `<DD>`)
`<ADDRESS></ADDRESS>`	address; often used for document author identification

Separators

`<H1></H1>... <H6></H6>`	headings from level 1 (major) to 6 (minor)
`<HR>`	horizontal rule
` `	line break
`<P>`	paragraph start (end paragraph, `</P>` optional)

Physical Character Formatting

`<B></B>`	**bold**
`<I></I>`	*italic*
`<TT></TT>`	`typewriter`
`<PRE></PRE>`	preformatted text; preserves line breaks

Logical Character Formatting

`<EM></EM>`	*emphasized*
`<STRONG></STRONG>`	**strongly emphasized**
`<KBD></KBD>`	keyboard entry
`<CITE></CITE>`	*citation*
`<VAR></VAR>`	*variable name*
`<SAMP></SAMP>`	text sample

Images

`<IMG Src="URL">`	inserts image at *URL* into document
`<IMG Src="URL" Alt="string">`	displays *string* for non-graphical browsers instead of image
`<IMG Src="URL" Align="top¦bottom¦middle">`	sets alignment of text after image

Forms

`<FORM Action="URL Method="get¦post"></FORM>`	a Form with a gateway program at *URL* and using a method
`<INPUT Name="name" Type="checkbox ¦hidden ¦image ¦password ¦radio ¦reset ¦submit ¦text">`	Input element with a specific type and symbolic name, *name*
`<TEXTAREA Name="name" Rows="R" Cols="C">`	Text area (lines of editable text) with symbolic name, *name* and *R* rows and *C* columns visible at a time
`<SELECT Name="name" Size="N" Multiple">`	Select element with symbolic name, *name, N* selections visible at a time; and multiple selections possible; selections defined using OPTION
`<OPTION Value="string">`	Option element used with SELECT; with returned value *string*

Tables

`<TABLE Border></TABLE>`	start and stop of a Table with a border
`<CAPTION></CAPTION>`	start and stop of the caption
`<TR></TR>`	start and stop of a row
`<TH Colspan="C" Rowspan="R"></TH>`	start and stop of a header cell spanning *C* columns and *R* rows
`<TD Colspan="C" Rowspan="R"></TD>`	start and stop of a data cell spanning *C* columns and *R* rows

Netscape Color Extensions

`<BODY Background="URL">`	sets background texture to image at *URL*
`<BODY Bgcolor="#RRGGBB">`	sets background to color with red, green, blue values given by hexidecimal
`RR, GG, BB <BODY Text="#RRGGBB">`	sets text color
`<BODY Link="#RRGGBB">`	sets unvisited links color
`<BODY VLink="#RRGGBB">`	sets visited links color
`<BODY ALink="#RRGGBB">`	sets active links color

See also:

- HTML Summary Information `http://www.rpi.edu/~decemj/pages/intro.html`
- WWW Consortium `http://www.w3.org/`
- WWW FAQ `http://sunsite.unc.edu/boutell/faq/www_faq.html`
- Web Developer's Library `http://www.stars.com/Vlib/`
- HTML Writer's Guild `http://www.mindspring.com/~guild/`

For more information on Web development, see *HTML and CGI Unleashed*, by John December, Mark Ginsburg, and chapter contributors in key areas. Indianapolis: Sams.net Publishing, 1995. ISBN 0-672-30745-6.

For more information on the World Wide Web, see *The World Wide Web Unleashed*, by John December, Neil Randall, and chapter contributors in key areas. Indianapolis: Sams.net Publishing, 1995. ISBN 0-672-30737-5.

To order either of these books, call Macmillan Computer Publishing 1(800)428-5331. For more information about the books, see the book support webs at `http://www.rpi.edu/~decemj/works/wdg.html` and `http://www.rpi.edu/~decemj/works/wwwu.html`.

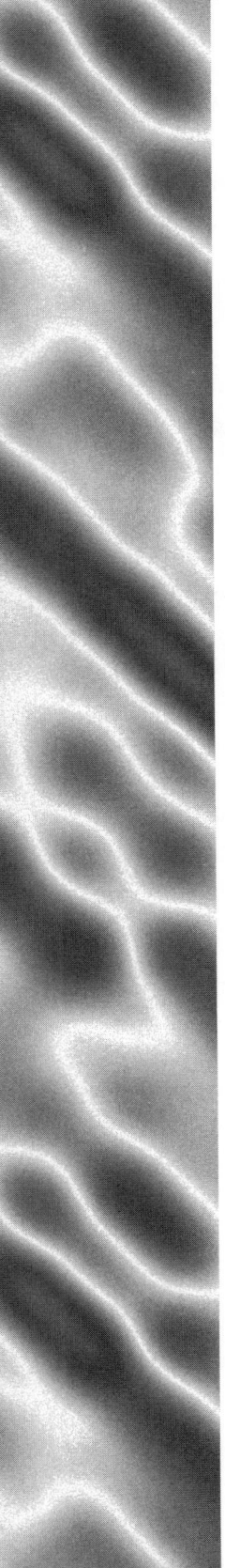

Glossary of Terms

anchor   A part of a hypertext document that is either the source or destination of a hypertext link. A link might extend from an anchor to another document, or from another document to an anchor. When anchors are the starting points of these links, they are typically highlighted or otherwise identified in the hypertext browser as hotspots.

ASCII   American Standard Code for Information Interchange. A 7-bit character code that can represent 128 characters, some of which are control characters used for communications control and are not printable.

applet   A Java program that can be included in an HTML page with the APP element and observed in a Java-enabled browser.

application (Java)   A stand-alone program, written in Java, that executes independently of the HotJava browser. This is done using the Java interpreter, java, included in the Java code distribution.

attribute   A property of an HTML element, specified in the start tag of the element. The attribute list of the APP element is used to pass values to the Java program defining the applet.

block (Java)   The code between matching curly braces { and }.

Boolean   A data type that has values true or false.

browser   A software program for observing the Web; a synonym for a Web client.

bytecode   The machine-readable code created as the result of compiling a Java language source file; this is the code distributed across the network to run an applet. Bytecodes are architecture neutral; the Java-capable browser ported to a particular platform interprets them.

cast (verb)   To change an expression from one data type to another.

child class   A subclass of a class (its parent class); it inherits public (and protected) data and methods from the parent class.

class   A template for creating objects; a class defines data and methods; a class is a unit of organization in a Java program. A class can pass on its public data and methods to its subclasses.

compiler   A software program that translates human-readable source code into machine-readable code.

constructor   A method named after its class. A constructor method is invoked when an object of that class is made.

content handler   A program loaded into the user's HotJava browser that interprets files of a type defined by the Java programmer. The Java programmer provides the necessary code for the user's HotJava browser to display/interpret this special format.

CPU   Central Processing Unit.

CERN (*Centre Europeen pour la Recherche Nucleaire*).   The European laboratory for particle physics, where the World Wide Web originated in 1989. (See `http://www.cern.ch/`.)

CGI (Common Gateway Interface)   A standard for programs to interface with Web servers.

client   A software program that requests information or services from another software application (server) and displays this information in a form required by its hardware platform.

DTD (Document Type Definition)   A specification for a markup language such as HTML to SGML.

domain name   The alphabetic name for a computer host; this name is mapped to the computer's numeric Internet Protocol (IP) address.

element   A unit of structure in an HTML document; many elements have start and stop tags; some have just a single tag; some elements can contain other elements.

FTP (File Transfer Protocol)   A means to exchange files across a network.

garbage collection   The process by which memory allocated for objects in a program is reclaimed. Java automatically performs this process.

Gopher   A protocol for disseminating information on the Internet using a system of menus.

hotspot   An area on a hypertext document that a user can click on to retrieve another resource or document.

HTML (Hypertext Markup Language)   The mechanism used to create Web pages; Web browsers display these pages according to a browser-defined rendering scheme.

HTTP (Hypertext Transfer Protocol)   The native protocol of the Web, used to transfer hypertext documents.

home page   An entry page for access to a local web; a page that a person or company defines as a principal page, often containing links to other pages containing personal or professional information.

HotJava   A Web browser designed to execute applets written in the Java programming language.

hypermedia   Hypertext that includes multimedia: text, graphics, images, sound, and video.

hypertext   Text that is not constrained to a single sequence for observation; Web-based hypertext is not constrained to a single server for creating meaning.

imagemap   A graphic inline image on an HTML page that potentially connects each pixel or region of an image to a Web resource; user mouse clicks on the image to retrieve the resources.

instance   An object.

interface   A set of methods that Java classes can implement.

Internet   The cooperatively run, globally distributed collection of computer networks that exchange information via the TCP/IP protocol suite.

Java   An object-oriented programming language for creating distributed, executable applications.

Java-enabled browser   A World Wide Web browser that can display Java applets.

link   A connection between one hypertext document and another.

method   A function that can perform operations on data.

MIME (Multipurpose Internet Mail Extensions)   A specification for multimedia document formats.

Matrix   The set of all networks that can exchange electronic mail either directly or through gateways. This includes the Internet, BITNET, FidoNet, UUCP, and commercial services such as America Online, CompuServe, Delphi, and Prodigy. This term was coined by John S. Quarterman in his book *The Matrix* (Digital Press, 1990).

Mosaic   A graphical Web browser originally developed by the National Center for Super-computing Applications (NCSA); now includes a number of commercially licensed products.

NCSA   National Center for Supercomputing Applications; at the University of Illinois at Urbana-Champaign; developers and distributors of NCSA Mosaic.

native methods   Class methods that are declared in a Java class but implemented in C.

navigating   The act of observing the content of the Web for some purpose.

Net, the   An informal term for the Internet or a subset (or a superset) of the Matrix in context. For example, a computerized conference via e-mail may take place on a BITNET host that has an Internet gateway, thus making the conference available to anyone on either of these networks. In this case, the developer might say, "Our conference will be available on the Net." One might even consider discussion forums on commercial online services to be "on the Net," although these are not accessible from the Internet.

object   A variable defined as being a particular class type. An object has the data and methods as specified in the class definition.

overload (verb)   To use the same name for several items in the same scope; Java methods can be overloaded.

packet   A set of data handled as a unit in data transmission.

package (Java)   A set of classes with a common high-level function declared with the `package` keyword.

page   A single file of hypertext markup language.

parameter list   The set of values passed to a method. The definition of the method describes how these values are manipulated.

parent class   The originating class of a given subclass.

protocol handler   A program that is loaded into the user's HotJava browser and that interprets a protocol. These protocols include standard ones such as HTTP or programmer-defined protocols.

robot   A term for software programs that automatically explore the Web for a variety of purposes; robots that collect resources for later database queries by users are sometimes called *spiders*.

scope   The program segment in which a reference to a variable is valid.

SGML (Standard Generalized Markup Language)   A standard for defining markup languages; HTML is an instance of SGML. (See `http://www.sgmlopen.org/`.)

server   A software application that provides information or services based on requests from client programs.

site   File section of a computer on which Web documents (or other documents served in another protocol) reside; for example, a Web site, a Gopher site, or an FTP site.

Solaris   Sun Microsystem's software platform for networked applications. Solaris includes an operating system, SunOS.

Sparc (Scalable Processor ARChitecture)   Based on a reduced instruction set computer (RISC) concept in which a microprocessor is designed for very efficient handling of a small set of instructions. (See `http://www.sparc.com/`.)

spider   A software program that traverses the Web to collect information about resources for later queries by users seeking to find resources; major species of active spiders include Lycos, WebCrawler.

surfing   The act of navigating the Web, typically using techniques for rapidly traversing the Web in order to find subjectively valuable resources.

tag   The format code used to make up part of an HTML element; for example, the `TITLE` element has a start tag, `<TITLE>` and an end tag, `</TITLE>`.

Unicode   A character set that supports many world languages.

URL (Uniform Resource Locator)   The scheme for addressing on the Web; a URL identifies a resource on the Web.

Usenet   A system for disseminating asynchronous text discussion among cooperating computer hosts; The Usenet discussion space is divided into newsgroups, each on a particular topic or subtopic.

TCP/IP (Transmission Control Protocol/Internet Protocol)   The set of protocols used for network communication on the Internet.

VRML (Virtual Reality Modeling Language)   A specification for three-dimensional rendering used in conjunction with Web browsers.

weaving   The act of creating and linking Web pages.

web   A set of hypertext pages that is considered a single work; typically, a single web is created by cooperating authors or an author and deployed on a single server with links to other servers; a subset of the Web.

Web (World Wide Web)   A hypertext information and communication system popularly used on the Internet computer network with data communications operating according to a client/server model. Web clients (browsers) can access multi-protocol and hypermedia information using an addressing scheme.

Web server   Software that provides the services to Web clients.

WWW   The World Wide Web.

X   X Window System; a windowing system supporting graphical user interfaces to applications.

See also:

- **C++ Glossary** (`http://info.desy.de/pub/uugna/html/cc/text/glossary/index.html`): This glossary lists terms related to the C++ language; because C++ is closely related to Java, these terms can also be helpful.

- **Sun's Java Glossary** (`http://java.sun.com/1.1alpha3/doc/misc/glossary.html`)

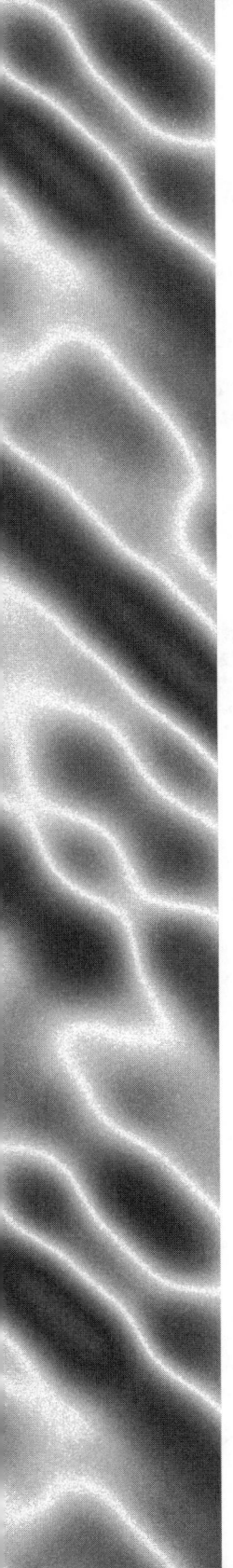

ndex

Add to Your Sams Library Today with the Best Books for Programming, Operating Systems, and New Technologies

The easiest way to order is to pick up the phone and call

1-800-428-5331

between 9:00 a.m. and 5:00 p.m. EST.
For faster service please have your credit card available.

ISBN	Quantity	Description of Item	Unit Cost	Total Cost
0-672-30737-5		The World Wide Web Unleashed, Second Edition	$39.99	
0-672-30714-6		The Internet Unleashed, Second Edition	$35.00	
0-672-30667-0		Teach Yourself Web Publishing with HTML in a Week	$25.00	
1-57521-005-3		Teach Yourself More Web Publishing with HTML in a Week	$29.99	
0-672-30764-2		Teach Yourself Web Publishing with Microsoft Word in a Week	$29.99	
0-672-30718-9		Navigating the Internet, Third Edition	$22.50	
1-57521-004-5		The Internet Business Guide, Second Edition	$25.00	
0-672-30595-X		Education on the Internet	$25.00	
0-672-30669-7		Plug-n-Play Internet	$35.00	
0-672-30765-0		Navigating the Internet with Windows 95	$25.00	
0-672-30719-7		Navigating the Internet with OS/2 Warp	$25.00	
❏ 3 ½" Disk		Shipping and Handling: See information below.		
❏ 5 ¼" Disk		TOTAL		

Shipping and Handling: $4.00 for the first book, and $1.75 for each additional book. Floppy disk: add $1.75 for shipping and handling. If you need to have it NOW, we can ship product to you in 24 hours for an additional charge of approximately $18.00, and you will receive your item overnight or in two days. Overseas shipping and handling adds $2.00 per book and $8.00 for up to three disks. Prices subject to change. Call for availability and pricing information on latest editions.

201 W. 103rd Street, Indianapolis, Indiana 46290

1-800-428-5331 — Orders   1-800-835-3202 — FAX   1-800-858-7674 — Customer Service

Book ISBN 1-57521-039-8

PLUG YOURSELF INTO...

MACMILLAN INFORMATION SUPERLIBRARY™

que

SAMS PUBLISHING

Hayden Books

que COLLEGE

NRP

alpha books

Brady

ADOBE PRESS

THE MACMILLAN INFORMATION SUPERLIBRARY™

Free information and vast computer resources from the world's leading computer book publisher—online!

FIND THE BOOKS THAT ARE RIGHT FOR YOU!

A complete online catalog, plus sample chapters and tables of contents give you an in-depth look at *all* of our books, including hard-to-find titles. It's the best way to find the books you need!

- **STAY INFORMED** with the latest computer industry news through our online newsletter, press releases, and customized Information SuperLibrary Reports.

- **GET FAST ANSWERS** to your questions about MCP books and software.

- **VISIT** our online bookstore for the latest information and editions!

- **COMMUNICATE** with our expert authors through e-mail and conferences.

- **DOWNLOAD SOFTWARE** from the immense MCP library:
    - Source code and files from MCP books
    - The best shareware, freeware, and demos

- **DISCOVER HOT SPOTS** on other parts of the Internet.

- **WIN BOOKS** in ongoing contests and giveaways!

TO PLUG INTO MCP: ➔

GOPHER: gopher.mcp.com

FTP: ftp.mcp.com

WORLD WIDE WEB: **http://www.mcp.com**

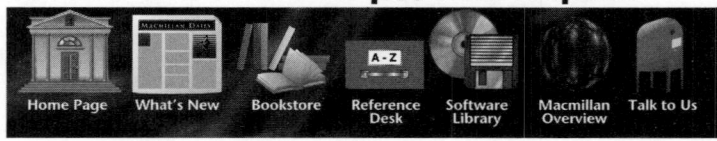

Home Page   What's New   Bookstore   Reference Desk   Software Library   Macmillan Overview   Talk to Us

Presenting Java Quick Reference

Sites

John December Book Support Sites
http://www.december.com/works/
Comments/questions to: john@december.com

Sun's Main Java Site
http://java.sun.com/
ftp://java.sun.com/

SunSITE's Mirror Java Site
http://sunsite.unc.edu/java/
ftp://sunsite.unc.edu/pub/languages/java/

An Essential Application

```
/**
 @author      john@december.com
 @version     1.34; 21 July 1995
 */
class EssentialApp {
    public static void main (String args[]) {
        System.out.println("Hello World!");
    }
}
```

An Essential Applet

```
import browser.Applet;
import awt.Graphics;
/**
 @author      john@december.com
 @version     1.01; 19 July 1995
 */
class EssentialApplet extends Applet {
    public void init() {
        resize(600, 300);
    }
    public void paint(Graphics context) {
        context.drawString("Hello, world!", 50, 100);
    }
}
```